Becoming Wife

To: Lauren

From: Leigh

Congrats!!
Wishing you a
lifetime of happiness

God Bless

Becoming Wife

SAYING YES TO MORE
THAN THE DRESS

RACHEL BULMAN

Our Sunday Visitor
Huntington, Indiana

Nihil Obstat
Msgr. Michael Heintz, Ph.D.
Censor Librorum

Imprimatur
✠Kevin C. Rhoades
Bishop of Fort Wayne-South Bend
January 31, 2023

The *Nihil Obstat* and *Imprimatur* are official declarations that a book is free from doctrinal or moral error. It is not implied that those who have granted the *Nihil Obstat* and *Imprimatur* agree with the contents, opinions, or statements expressed.

Our Sunday Visitor Publishing Division, Our Sunday Visitor, Inc., 200 Noll Plaza, Huntington, IN 46750; 1-800-348-2440; www.osv.com

ISBN: 978-1-68192-686-5 (Inventory No. T2560)
1. RELIGION—Christian Living—Love & Marriage.
2. RELIGION—Christian Living—Women's Interests.
3. RELIGION—Christianity—Catholic.

eISBN: 978-1-68192-687-2
LCCN: 2023933777

Cover design: Tyler Ottinger
Cover art: AdobeStock
Interior design: Amanda Falk
Interior art: AdobeStock

PRINTED IN THE UNITED STATES OF AMERICA

This book is dedicated to my husband, Jason, for makng me a wife. The yeses we gave to one another have changed the world. And to the wives of the 2022 permanent diaconate cohort in Orlando — our conversations started the thoughts that formed this book. Thank you.

Contents

Introduction

He who loves his wife loves himself.
— Ephesians 5:28

He who finds a wife finds a good thing,
and obtains favor from the Lord.
— Proverbs 18:22

If you're preparing to be a wife, you're likely going to pre-Cana classes, thinking about where you will live, picking out wedding details, planning the honeymoon, and more. If you're already a wife, you might be rearing children, working a job outside the home, trying to keep the house clean, managing multiple calendars, and even more than that. There's so much focus on the exterior life of being a wife: What will I do? What do I do now? How will I do it? When will I do it? And very little focus on the *interior* life of being a wife: Who am I? Who am I called to be?

There is absolutely no chance that being a wife is insignificant. This yes of your vow at the altar is shaped by your yeses before it, and further, shapes every yes afterward.

The writer of Proverbs deems the wife so important that her presence gains favor for the man who chooses her (see Prv 18:22). That same writer later writes almost an entire chapter on what it looks like to be the woman who takes care of her spouse, her children, and her home (Prv 31). But what about the heart of that woman? How do I become the type of wife who wins favor for her spouse and for her entire household? The answer involves much more than keeping a to-do list and balancing multiple schedules.

Being a wife is a call to holiness, a call which unfolds with every decision you make in this life. Becoming wife is the beginning of this unfolding, and within matrimony you can become more and more "wife," thereby gaining more and more favor. Your becoming even enables those around you to become more and more holy, more and more of who *they* are called to be.

When I look back on the memory of my husband, Jason, kneeling before me to ask me to be his wife, I realize that moment was another beginning for me. The yes

I spoke then was a continuation of my yes as a daughter of God. It didn't negate who I had been, but added to who I am. I became daughter even more, in a new way, and at the same time began becoming wife.

• • •

I always knew I would be a wife. Maybe you could blame the lack of vocation talk in my Protestant upbringing or my ignorance in any other available paths, but nevertheless, I've always thought that married life was for me. Despite the lies our culture tells us and the failed marriages I had seen in my own family, I was somehow granted the grace to still believe that authentic love and a happy marriage were possible.

I've been married to Jason for over almost fifteen years. We have welcomed six children into the world and lost one before we could meet him. I converted to Catholicism before we got engaged, and together we discerned his call to the permanent diaconate. After six years in formation, he received the Sacrament of Holy Orders. It was an interesting and beautiful ride, and all along the way the Lord generously laid before me a call to become a better wife.

The little girl who creates weddings with her dolls and the teenager who saves all her favorite "big day" details to a secret Pinterest board never imagine that formation is needed for becoming a wife. We slip the ring on, we plan the day of our dreams, and we ride off into the sunset. But what does it mean to become a wife?

We should talk about that. There are piles of books on being a child of God, on finding one's filial identity, especially as a daughter. There are many books on being a holy and loving mother, on rearing children to become saints. Most of the books on being a wife are only in conjunction with the husband — rightly so, since a wife is only a wife because she is spouse to her husband. But there is still much to be explored about who a wife is. There is so much weight on this part of a woman's life that many times she changes her last name, where she lives, even how she spends her time.

As we become spouse, our happiness as wives is found within this relationship. This marriage is not the husband's joy alone but his joined with mine. When I pick up laundry that somehow missed the basket, when I prepare a meal for the family, when I awaken in the middle of the night to a crying child or a snoring husband (he swears he doesn't snore), when I say yes to the mundane realities of marriage over and over again, I am taken back to the moment my husband knelt before me and I revisit that fiat. *Yes, I will serve you. Yes, I will suffer with you. Yes, I will rejoice with you. Yes, I will be your wife.*

Answering this particular call to holiness requires that I give myself as gift. There is no objectification in this gift. True gift cannot be objectified. We will wade through those hazy waters together too. No, this gift as wife is a surrender to the other for the sake of the other only to inevitably find yourself in his gaze.

When Jason and I first met, I would often catch him staring at me. It would drive me crazy, and not in a good way! I'd look back at him and ask, slightly annoyed, "Why are you looking at me?" He would laugh and reply, "I think you're beautiful." And I'd tell him to stop. There was nothing sexual or objectifying in his gaze. He was so free in loving me that it made me uncomfortable. I hated it! I realized later that I hated it because part of me was uncomfortable with the idea that anyone could love me simply for me — with no expectations or ulterior motives.

After a decade of marriage, I was sitting in prayer for him and realized that I hadn't felt that gaze in a while. I started to question myself and him until I asked the Lord, "Why doesn't Jason look at me like that anymore? Have I lost his loving gaze?" Almost as clearly as I type these words now, I felt the Lord reply, "Oh he still does, but now *you believe him.*"

This is my desire in writing this book. For you, preparing to become someone's wife; or you, considering that one day you may meet the man you are to marry; or you who are still in the newlywed stages of matrimony; or even you, the wife of many years rediscovering your vocation. You can find happiness here, in this book and in your marriage, because you are beloved. The gaze of your spouse is the gaze in which shame disappears. There is nothing small about being a wife. It's not a blip on the timeline of becoming holy, or a series of new obstacles you'll have to surmount to reach holiness. Becoming wife requires an entire change in the vision of what becoming holy actually is. That vow on the altar is the first time that you audibly, physically, emotionally, mentally, and entirely say yes to becoming gift to another, and through that gift discover a deeper understanding of God's love for you and his desire for your heart.

Together we will discuss the divine and human reality of spousality. With that foundation, we will expand our understanding of what saying yes really means and how the period of engagement deserves much more attention than we give it. We are going to discuss the hard things too, such as, What does it really mean to be "open to life"? How can I love my spouse without losing myself in that love? How does healing interplay with the Sacrament of Matrimony? And we will talk about how good and holy marriages are in and of themselves part of the new evangelization, and how being a wife requires us to be a child first.

Let's dive deep into spaces in your heart, some of which you might be familiar with and others you didn't know existed. We will unwrap the gift that you are and shine a light on how that gift is further discovered as a wife. You should pause as frequently as you can, allowing yourself to reflect on provoking passages and how they affect your marriage or your preparation for marriage. You'll hear my thoughts on being a wife, but we will also share this space with saints and others pursuing holiness with us.

If being or becoming a wife is not in your future,

even if you desire it, I still think you will find something within these pages. Spousality is a reality for every person, and the manifestation of it comes in more than just the form of being a wife. You will still practice many of the things that we explore in this book — dying to self for the sake of the other, healing, cooperating with the call of Christ, and more. If you never have children, you will still be fully wife, and will be given other ways to practice parenthood in a more spiritual sense. If your husband doesn't understand why you would read such a book, and your call to being and becoming wife seems like a lonely journey without a husband who wants to reciprocate or participate, you will still find solace in these pages — for your wounds, for your desires, and for your call.

May these pages affirm you, convert you, and guide you in your journey as wife. Don't forget to take your husband with you. Your happiness and his has been found in your yes.

Why Spousality
Matters

You are made in the image and likeness of God.

You've probably heard that before, or its Latin equivalent, *imago dei* (pronounced ee-mah-go day-ee). I had never heard that phrase before I became Catholic, and now I know it's more than just a phrase — it's a fact, an innate reality of the human person. But it's played out, right? That sentence can be chalked up there with other overused buzzwords: "Jesus loves you," "What would Jesus do?" "Feminine Genius." In fact, when I hear these overused phrases, bumper stickers, and bracelet slogans, I tend to tune out. But these phrases are more than bumper stickers; they are incredibly powerful truths.

Imago dei, that truth that we are made in the image and likeness of God, is a life-changing reality found in Scripture and carried through our tradition by great minds like Saint Irenaeus, Tertullian, Saint Augustine, and St. Thomas Aquinas. In more recent years, the Second Vatican Council re-presented it throughout its documents but most notably in the Pastoral Constitution *Gaudium et Spes* (Joy and Hope). Pope St. John Paul II and Pope Benedict XVI spoke of *imago dei* frequently in their writings, too.

Irenaeus taught that "image" is ontological, an intrinsic part of human nature, while "likeness" is realized or denied by moral decision. Tertullian followed suit, teaching that the image can never be destroyed but our likeness to God can be lost by sin. Two hundred years later, Augustine expanded the teaching on *imago dei*, explaining that we are naturally oriented toward God, and this orientation is maintained and realized through prayer, knowledge, and love. Further still, Aquinas introduced three stages of *imago dei*: one received when we are created (*imago creationis*), another when we are redeemed through salvation (*imago recreationis*), and finally one when we are united with God in heaven (*imago similitudinis*). Aquinas also affirmed that while *imago dei* is an ontological reality, we must participate with it.

Genesis 1:27 says, "So God created man in his own image, / in the image of God he created him; / male and female he created them." Because I grew up steeped in Scripture, this verse was not foreign to me, but its gravity was. After the Reformation, the truth of *imago dei* continued through Protestant theology, but aspects of the teaching were distorted or lost altogether, particularly the ontological reality of image. Likeness remained but could only be achieved through personal relationship. I thought that I needed to create an image from scratch, but how can a painter paint a picture without an image in mind or a model to mimic?

Saint Athanasius wrote *On the Incarnation* in the fourth century, and explains the answer to my question. He says, "A portrait once effaced must be restored from the original. Thus the Son of the Father came to seek, save, and regenerate. No other way was possible. Blinded himself, man could not see to heal. The witness of creation had failed to preserve him, and could not bring him back. The Word alone could do so. But how? Only by revealing himself as Man."*

I'm not a painter re-creating an image without a model. Instead, made in the image of God though marred by sin, I am restored when placed next to and in right relationship with the one in whom my image and likeness is found.

Another example of image and likeness plays itself out in my own life. I was adopted when I was very young, and though my adoptive parents are a different nation-

---

*"Essay," in *Nicene and Post-Nicene Fathers*, second series, ed. Philip Schaff and Henry Wace, vol. 4, *Athanasius: Select Works and Letters* (Peabody, MA: Hendrickson Publishers, 1995), 43.

ality from me, we are still in the same image. We are still human persons, sharing the image of our humanity. On the other hand, our likeness has been realized through relationship. I have become more and more like them because of our relationship. I talk like them. I share their mannerisms and family traditions. I am like them because of my relationship to them.

In *Gaudium et Spes*, the Church unpacks the implications of *imago dei*: "The truth is that only in the mystery of the incarnate Word does the mystery of man take on light" (no. 22). With these words, we are reminded that when God became man, his life and death revealed so much about us. Simple things are made extraordinary when seen through the light of the Incarnation.

In my life, I am simultaneously a child, a wife, and a mother. I have learned so much about myself and about God through these different relationships, and firmly believe that every person is called to them — to be child, to be spouse, and to be parent. There are situations where these relationships are not possible in the biological sense, but those situations do not diminish the call. For instance, my adoption does not include the biological sense of being a child, but it doesn't make me less child. A widow is still a spouse, and a married couple that cannot conceive often answer the call to be parent in many other ways. These are the patterns of humanity: child, spouse, and parent — in other words, anthropological patterns.

If we take these patterns and place them next to the

divine, Trinitarian life of God, we can identify the theological patterns of the person as well.

Trinitarian Love

One of my favorite images of the Trinity shows a bearded and aged God the Father with his arms extended in front of him, palms up. In those arms hangs the crucified Christ, God the Son, with his outstretched arms held up by the Father's arms. Above the head of the Father is a dove, the Holy Spirit. The Father is pouring himself out for the Son, while the Son pours himself out for mankind and simultaneously entrusts himself to the Father. Out of this mutual self-gift we see the Holy Spirit, abiding with the Father and the Son.

> *The Father is being for. The Son is being from. The Holy Spirit is being with. And these methods of being are also expressed in the human person.*

Pope Benedict XVI called these relationships between the persons of the Trinity "methods of being." The Father is being *for*. The Son is being *from*. The Holy Spirit is being *with*. And these methods of being are also expressed in the human person. As a child, the person is being *from*. As a spouse, the person is being *with*. As a parent, the person is being *for*.

Love, that desire for the good of the other, always

exists as for, with, from. We are for the other, with the other, and from the other. How does this inform the understanding we have of ourselves?

Throughout our lives we face the reality of these modes of love. We are born and thus, *from* someone. We are a part of families and communities. We are *with* one another. We find vocations, devote our lives to missions and ministries, become spouses and parents. We learn to live *for* the other.

Many books could be written on each of these forms of love. If you go to your local bookstore or do a quick Amazon search, you'll find scores of books on understanding our identity as children of God. After all, this is the primary, the first identity of the person. We must be child before we can be anything else! And if you search for books on parenthood, you'll find even more resources. But books on spousality, being *with* and *for* through being wife, are scarce — which is why we are exploring this topic together.

What does it mean to be *with*, to mirror the communion of the Holy Spirit? What are we talking about when we use this word *spousality*?

Shared Likeness

First and foremost, when a man and woman are called to marriage, their union is based on a shared, common existence. There is something in the other that draws them — a recognition that the other is *like* them. Within the truth that "it is not good that the man should be alone" (Gn 2:18), God created woman from man so that they share the same likeness to one another but also to God.

The scene that plays out in the book of Genesis is quite beautiful. Adam was given the task of naming each animal in the garden. But as Adam identified the creatures of the Garden, he knew that he did not share his likeness with them. I imagine him touching and inspecting every animal, giving them names and identifying how they would be known from that point on, but also realizing that this giraffe, this monkey, this animal is not like him. He was alone, but he was also alone with God. Pope St. John Paul II called this "original solitude," something that only human persons are capable of.

Adam falls asleep alone, but when he wakes up, he finds a world renewed, where he is no longer by himself. Eve is the first creation that he sees and immediately finds joy and gladness in her existence. He accepts her as like him, one who looks like him, whose heart is like his own, and who is also called to be loved just as he is called to be loved. She not only shares his likeness in body and stature but also something more: She shares his original solitude, this ability to be alone with God.

Today, that same story plays out for those of us called into marriage. It seems almost like a fairy tale — we went to sleep alone, but we open our eyes to a new world that is shared. Nothing new exists, other than seeing this other person who has existed all along, but the newness resides in the gaze of love, one to the other, and even more, in being seen together by the gaze of God who is love itself. This gaze can be uncomfortable at first, but can envelop us like a blanket when we have the freedom to be loved and warmed by it.

Cardinal Joseph Ratzinger, later Pope Benedict XVI, wrote, "The Father and the Son are one with each other by going out beyond themselves; it is in the third Person, in the fruitfulness of their act of giving, that they are One."* You could say that Jason and I were individuals until we went out of ourselves and toward each other to become one.

The Call to Faithful Love

Second, the mutual admiration of a husband and wife calls them into *love*. This may seem like an obvious note. Of course, we are called into love! But we must realize simultaneously that if love is from God, and God is love, then we are participating, as spouses, in the truth summarized in the creed: "God from God." Made in his image and likeness, we hand on that image and likeness to each other. Through our ability to see and be seen, we either sharpen the vision of this likeness or we mar the image of God in the other.

Proverbs 27:17 says, "Iron sharpens iron, / and one man sharpens another." The original Hebrew uses the word "face": "One person sharpens the face of another." In other words, every interaction between spouses is like a lens given to each other to see oneself and the world.

---

*Joseph Ratzinger, "The Holy Spirit as *Communio*," 171.

We either pass on a clear view of our spouse through the lens of Christ's love, or we pass on a blurry, diminished version of our spouse, displacing their innate beloved-ness through a dull and marred lens. In order to pass on a clear view, we must have a clear view of ourselves, avoiding the temptation to allow the "blind to lead the blind."

This call to love is so grave that it must be an abiding love, a constant love. In order to be *with*, we must be with *always*, for the responsibility of "God from God" requires the promise to stay, to accompany, and to endure. Love is meant to be forever. This is the call to fidelity. Our mutual admiration must be realized and cultivated. If it is not, the admiration of one spouse can become distracted and cause damage to the promise of fidelity.

The Call to Gift

Finally, and the most pertinent aspect to becoming wife, the spouse is called to be *gift* to the other. Let's be honest, who doesn't love gifts? And you, my friend, are a gift, to be cherished, adored, and received.

Think of the action of giving someone a gift. My oldest daughter, Gemma, was very excited to pick out a gift for a friend's upcoming birthday party. Gemma asked her at school about her wishes and came home with a list of ten gifts we "needed" to pick up for her best friend. I explained that we shouldn't get all the gifts because we needed to allow others to buy some of them. Thankfully, this satisfied her, and we picked out two gifts to bring to her friend. She wrapped them up, and when Gemma gave the gift at the party, her anticipation of her friend's joy was nearly palpable. Her posture while choosing the gift, wrapping it, and then giving it to her friend was one of excitement and joy. This is the perfect imagery of what being *for* can be like — giving of oneself completely for the fulfillment of the other, for their joy, and for their care. In doing so, we discover our own heart overcome with delight.

Being a spouse calls us into this vulnerable and visible place of giving ourselves and being seen. We give what we have to the other. Their reception of our gift not only affirms the reality that we are worthy of being gift, but also multiplies and expands our gift beyond self-imposed limitations. Gemma was tempted to think that if she gave her friend a large quantity of gifts, it would result in an increase of love from her friend, but later realized that the capacity of the gift was not determined by quantity but by the mere act of it being given. You could even say that the desire to give is greater than the gift itself, an authentic understanding of "it's the thought that counts." Giving the gift must be more about the receiver than the giver so that the giving is truly oriented outward and not toward oneself. When we are turned inward, our vision is selfish, drawn toward ourselves, and our generosity is limited. But when we focus on the other, our eyes drift outward. We see beyond ourselves and into the great abundance of being gift.

A Lifelong Journey

When we respond to the call of being wife, we are saying yes to all these things: yes to likeness, yes to love, yes to forever, and yes to being and receiving gift. While each of these tasks seems so easy in theory, the difficulty lies in their endlessness. Your commitment is not a once-and-done deal. You don't say yes at the altar and then the rest falls magically into place. You say yes to this state of life as wife and you repeat that yes throughout your marriage, day in and day out. On the one hand, you are in a static place of being wife, but you are also in a dynamic state of becoming, of becoming more and more gift, more and more love, and more and more like God.

Pope St. John Paul II said in *Love and Responsibility*, "For love is never something ready made, something merely 'given' to man and to women, it is always at the same time a 'task' which they are set." He continued, "Love should be seen as something which in a sense never 'is' but is always only 'becoming', and what it becomes depends upon the contribution of both persons and the depth of their commitment."* This reminds us that marriage is not a destination, but instead a lifelong journey toward becoming who we are called to be. While a man and woman are given to each other in the Sacrament of Matrimony, they become spouse and spend the rest of their lives becoming more and more spouse. The ability to become is thus dependent on both man and wom-

---

*Karol Wojtyła, *Love and Responsibility* (San Francisco: Ignatius Press, 1993), 139.

an, on their depth of commitment to each other and the sacrament, as well as their desire to progress toward love forever and always.

Growing in the likeness of God — again manifested in the reality of marriage, of *being with and being for* — is found in the ongoing exchange of the gift of matrimony between man and woman.

When Scripture says, "So God created man in his own image, / in the image of God he created him; / male and female he created them" (Gn 1:27), it speaks of a singular God creating singularly. But the second part of this verse changes the subject of that creation — "in the image of God he created them." Thus, a singular God creates all mankind as men and as women, as male and female.

While our likeness to God is given through our humanity, it is further revealed through sexuality. So when man and woman marry, becoming husband and wife, their total gift of self reveals a clearer understanding of their own *imago dei*. Because the *imago* is both male and female, the unity of the two makes that image sharper. The *Catechism* says, "In no way is God in man's image. He is neither man nor woman. ... But the respective 'perfections' of man and woman reflect something of the infinite perfection of God" (CCC 370). So, we see the image of God clearer because of the glimpses that we see in our lives as husband and wife. In our marriages, we witness love and goodness. While finite compared to God who is love and goodness himself, the love and goodness in our marriages reveals more about who God is and what the *imago* looks like.

Mary as Bride

Where else do we see the relationship between man and woman sharpening the image of God in the other? In the life of the Blessed Virgin Mary, who will be our constant companion on our journey of becoming wife. She is the bride of Joseph, the bride of the Holy Spirit, and mother of the Church, which is the Bride of Christ. To be the bride, she must exemplify one thing: radical openness.

Mary is in a constant state of receiving in order to give whatever she receives back to the Creator. Even at the Annunciation, her questioning ("How will this be, since I do not know man?" [Lk 1:34]) is a journey toward understanding. She believes in God's plan for her and desires to receive the truth given to her ("And behold, you will conceive in your womb and bear a son" [Lk 1:31]). Inevitably, the miracle of the Incarnation occurs at the point where rationality and faith meet. This small instance of questioning displays Mary's desire to understand so she can fully receive what is given to her and thus give it back by bearing the child Jesus within her womb.

"Let it be to me according to your word" (Lk 1:38) is an incredibly strenuous and extreme "traditional" view of woman — the exact opposite of the modern-day feminist movement. For the modern-day feminist, power is incorrectly synonymous with office or the ability to control. Where women seek this false power, there is a grave temptation to become more like man attempting to wield it, thereby diminishing their gender or completely abandoning the genius of their femininity all together. Instead, the Annunciation presents a woman whose radical openness is not confined to some false ideal of 1950s homemaking, where the housewife is seen caring for the household in such a way that any sign of effort is erased. Her slaving over dinner must appear effortless and the kitchen must be cleaned immaculately. When the husband comes home from work, she must be in an ankle length skirt with perfectly coiffed hair and attractive makeup, erasing all the work of the day that might be found in the bags under her eyes or the spit-up on her blouse. In this mind-set, women are tempted to erase their feminine genius because of the lie that femininity must mean outward perfection.

Our Lady was certainly not a woman who hid the strenuous reality of radical openness. I'm sure that giving birth to her child inside a stable didn't include sweet-smelling candles and perfectly coiffed hair. Nor were her years of keeping her home in Nazareth always picture-perfect and without strain. Her heart was pierced at the presentation of Our Lord in the temple, and she suffered with her Son on Calvary. A pierced heart certainly translated to her face, to her body. There is no erasing or covering up a life lived in radical openness.

Mary, who is the woman who is most open, most holy, and most in line with the will of God, did not rely on her own capabilities. She didn't bask in the conception of the Messiah alone but shared it with her cousin Elizabeth. She didn't journey to Bethlehem alone but was taken through the love of Saint Joseph. She entrusted herself to the guidance of her earthly spouse. In fact, it is precisely through spousal love that God reveals his love to the world by the Incarnation, and that being with and being for, loves and nurtures Christ his entire life.

A large part of becoming wife and radically opening yourself is to give into the limits, even the frailty, of your person. It's not that your husband completes you, but that he is a soft place to land. He should provide a haven for you, but there is no haven if you are not willing to be sequestered there. That radical surrender of Our Lady was not a passive existence. She was steadfast and decisive in her surrender to the will of God. She received the news of the Archangel and later, when the baby that she had received had grown into a man, she helped to initiate his public ministry at the wedding at Cana. Her radical surrender allowed her to avoid the extremes in which many women find themselves today — extreme independence or extreme dependence.

Radical Openness

I'm a huge fan of women's empowerment until "power" is used to manipulate reality. Our power truly lies in our femininity. I must own my femininity and all the talents, gifts, likes, and dislikes that come along with it. I cannot wield any of my talents or gifts as weapons nor should I give any of them up in pursuit of some masculine genius that I do not have in order to become "successful." And I can never be independent in its strictest sense because I am a being in need of communion. At the other extreme is dependence. If you look up the opposite of *independence* in the thesaurus, you'll find *dependence* but also *subservient* — which immediately makes me think of that often-misinterpreted verse from Ephesians 5:22. We often get so heated about that verse that we forget about the verse before it: "Be subject to *one another* out of reverence for Christ."

Dependence, in the way that the world sees it, sets us up for crippling reliance on the other and ultimately loss of self. Dependence in this way becomes weakness, unless we redefine weakness through the life of Christ. God bound himself to his own creation by becoming man. He no longer identifies himself apart from his Bride, the Church. They are bound together and his mission is only accomplished through her. God who is all-powerful does not choose to operate in a hermeneutic of power; instead he gives himself in radical vulnerability.

Often we reject radical openness, which requires us to be deeply vulnerable, due to a fear of being hurt. So we bind our love up in a box unwilling to share freely because vulnerability costs, it risks. This reminds me of one of my favorite quotes from C. S. Lewis's *Four Loves*, a quote we'll come back to several times:

> To love at all is to be vulnerable. Love anything and your heart will be wrung and possibly broken. If you want to make sure of keeping it intact you must give it to no one, not even an animal. Wrap it carefully round with hobbies and little luxuries; avoid all entanglements. Lock it up safe in the casket or coffin of your selfishness. But in that casket, safe, dark, motionless, airless, it will change. It will not be broken; it will become unbreakable, impenetrable, irredeemable.*

To love is to be vulnerable.

But how can we love vulnerably while maintaining our selfhood, our independence? We must live in the tension of being dependent upon the other and being independent of the other for the sake of communion. Being in communion requires another outside of myself.

Becoming wife means maintaining the tension that lies between the extremes of dependence and independence. We must learn to serve but also to allow ourselves to be served. We have to exercise our God-given talents, charisms, and strengths while allowing our husbands to exercise theirs. When we choose to embrace this tension, we are less vulnerable to the temptation of self-creation which is found in extreme independence, and the

---

* C. S. Lewis, *The Four Loves* (New York: Harcourt Books, 1960), PAGE

loss of self found in dependence. Your difference from your spouse allows for communion. You do not have to become like your husband to be loved by him or to have a happy marriage. The unity of man and woman in marriage gives each spouse a responsibility to call each other into being more than themselves. Jason wants me to be Rachel, and I want him to be Jason. We answer the call to self-gift, transcending our self-fascination and utter dependence by maintaining that which makes us each unique while appreciating the uniqueness in the other.

> *We have to exercise our God-given talents, charisms, and strengths while allowing our husbands to exercise theirs.*

Spousality and Gift

In this sincere gift of self we discover who we are. Let's return to *Gaudium et Spes*:

> Indeed, the Lord Jesus, when he prayed to the Father, "that all may be one … as we are one" (Jn 17:21–22) opened up vistas closed to human reason, for he implied a certain likeness between the union of the divine Persons, and the unity of God's sons in truth and charity. This likeness reveals that man, who is the only crea-

ture on earth which God willed for itself, cannot fully find himself except through a sincere gift of himself. (no. 24)

Spousality recognizes who we are without discouraging our uniqueness. Spouses must maintain their individuality to also maintain their communion. In this way, we mirror the Trinitarian life of God. The three persons of the Trinity are three persons for the sake of communion, who are constantly pouring themselves out for the other. I do not lose who I am when I become wife, but instead, through relationship, become more and more myself.

Spousality also calls us into fidelity, and we are given the charge to call one another into our *imago dei*. It is a reality of being gift, complete and total gift; of radical openness; and of maintaining the tension between dependence and independence. We remain who we are in order to celebrate the union of persons, and there's a particular call for the wife in every aspect of spousality which always begins with saying yes.

As the persons of the Trinity actualize the modes of being *for* (God the Father), being *from* (God the Son), and being *with* (God the Holy Spirit), we respond to a call to image each of those modes in our lives — and we rely on the Trinity to show us what it is to be child, spouse, and parent. Just as it is impossible to speak about one aspect of the Trinity without talking about the others, we too have to avoid the temptation to skip that mode that doesn't seem to apply to me today or the mode that I don't quite understand.

If you skip over spousality, you will have a harder time being a parent. Notice I did not say it is impossible, only harder. In fact, when I'm frustrated with parenting, I find solace within my marriage and then further solace in my identity as a child of God. This is a perpetual cycle in life — child, spouse, and parent — actualized by the sacramental life of the Church. We become child through the Sacrament of Baptism, spouse and often parent through the Sacrament of Matrimony. The role of parenthood is not realized right away, but the possibility of such fecundity is sealed within the Sacrament of Matrimony, hidden within your spousality (see CCC 1652–1654).

One final note: Parenthood is a part of every person's life. It may not be the way we imagined — with children running around at our feet who share our genes and our physical likeness. It can happen in other ways — through adoption, for example, a gift which made me a child to my adoptive parents. It can also happen through spiritual mentorship, through friendship and community, and through caring for others who have entrusted themselves to your heart. You become a parent to children (and adults) who share your heart, share your likeness through relationship, and who know they are beloved children of God because you've shared this valuable truth with them. I have many more spiritual sons and daughters than I do physical ones, and I pray that you do too.

Saying Yes

I can still remember the night that Jason asked me to marry him. He was in physician-assistant school, and I was living a few hours away. We had been spending a lot of time apart because of his schedule with classes and studying. He called one day and asked me out to dinner: "Let's have a nice night together since it's been so long."

The day of our reservation, he took me to a local mall and told me I should find a dress and shoes. I really thought nothing of it. That shopping trip was likely the longest shopping trip of both our lives. Even though I had no idea what was about to take place, I wanted to find the perfect outfit, which is no easy feat! Jason knew what he had planned and had to keep a particular schedule for the night. You can see how this didn't work out for us since he couldn't lie and say that the first outfit looked great, or pressure me to hurry up so we wouldn't miss our reservation. That kind of coaxing is part of my character (sadly) but not part of his (thankfully). And yes, we were late for our reservation.

Jason had spent months, with his father's help, trying to figure out the perfect place to ask me to be his wife. His plan was to take me to dinner at a swanky hotel and explore the gardens around the property since, of course, we would get there with plenty of time left for a tour and the all-important question. He had even chosen the perfect spot where he would kneel down and ask me to be his wife. But Plan A didn't work out.

We had a beautiful dinner. The restaurant was just a few minutes away from Downtown Disney, and since it was the Fourth of July weekend, we were going to go and watch the fireworks display. Jason's back-up plan was to ask me to marry him while the fireworks were going off, but the normally five-minute drive took half an hour with holiday traffic. Given the traffic and already being behind schedule, we both thought the fireworks would be long over when we arrived.

We finally got into Downtown Disney and ducked into a little restaurant to grab a drink. Jason guided me over to a quiet corner sofa and exasperated he said, "I've been trying to say something to you all night long."

I thought he was going to break up with me! How cruel would that have been to have me dress up, take me to a nice dinner, and then dump me at Downtown Disney?! Thankfully, I was extremely wrong that night, and these days my worst-case-scenario mentality is long gone.

Jason continued, "You have made me one of the happiest men in the world, and I know that you would make me a great husband and a great father."

He reached into his pocket, took out a ring, and knelt down on one knee in front of me. I laughed uncomfortably and said, "You better not be joking!"

Then he asked me to be his wife.

As I said yes, we heard a loud pop outside and the fireworks were just beginning. Literally, and figuratively.

The moment you're asked to spend your life with your beloved is a moment many of you won't forget. We vividly remember the anticipation, the preparation, the feelings in that moment. We spend ample time looking back at how the evening unfolded, laughing at how the surprise worked out or how the night went awry. But ultimately, if it works out, if she says yes, that evening is the beginning of something new.

There was a time when I wanted the song "God Bless the Broken Road" to be played for our first dance. The refrain of that song alludes to the fact that all the failed relationships lead you to the love you have now. What a beautiful sentiment!

I think saying yes to marriage is that way. Your assent, your affirmation of this other person, is like wrapping your arms around him. As your arms extend, you also pull into this embrace all his past and all his future. In the yes of this present moment, everything before it led me here and everything after it will be seen through this yes. It is not a division between your single self and your betrothed/married self, but is instead a continuation of who you are by expanding within self-gift. From birth to life, you are increasing your openness by your yes to the other.

Every yes is an echo of the yes of our Blessed Mother.

Every yes is an echo of the yes of our Blessed Mother. Like her yes, our yes to becoming wife is a renunciation of what the world has to offer and a yes to something beyond this world.

Reject the World's Lies about Marriage

More and more, people are waiting much later to get married or saying no to marriage all together. *The Knot 2020 Real Wedding Study* surveyed twenty-five hundred couples who were married in 2019. It revealed that the average age of marriage is thirty-one for women and thirty-three for men. It suggests several reasons for this statistic:

- The brain doesn't fully develop until age twenty-five.

- People are taking longer to find themselves.
- People are working.*

Your yes to marriage is a renunciation of these explanations. The truth is that while brain development, finding oneself, and having a job might deter men and women from the commitment of marriage, it doesn't have to be this way.

At the young age of nine and ten, my sons began to delineate some truths that even the greatest saints took a lifetime to understand. Perhaps the focus on the "fully developed brain" is another result of our modern fragmentation of the human person. Your brain, which affects the way you understand the world and make choices, has a lot to do with your soul; and an underdeveloped soul will delay intellectual development too. Understanding and living the virtues is not a task only for the aged. It is a task for the human in every stage of development.

In addition, brain development is not synonymous with intelligence, and intelligence is not synonymous with living the virtues. I think we can all agree that we are all still learning (and unlearning) after the age of twenty-five. I also know young people who are smart people, and smart people who are not virtuous. Thus, the claim that the brain is fully developed at age 25 cannot be a good reason for people to wait to get married.

I think the last two claims can be refuted together.

---

*https://www.wedinsights.com/report/covid-the-knot-real-weddings

In the previous chapter, I wrote about our likeness to God and the communal nature of God in Three Persons, which lay the foundation for understanding this line from *Gaudium et Spes*: "This likeness reveals that man, who is the only creature on earth which God willed for itself, cannot fully find himself except through a sincere gift of himself" (no. 24).

When I get an opportunity to ask young people why they aren't married yet, they always have the same litany of answers. They want to travel more, save up more money, get established in their job, or meet goal x, y, or z. They presuppose that doing those things will somehow make them more ready to enter into matrimony. But it also highlights the common mistake of placing our worth or our identity in something else:

- I'll be ready for marriage once I've traveled to three countries.
- If I have at least $10,000 in my savings account, I'll be ready for marriage.
- As soon as that promotion comes through, I can walk down the aisle.

None of these goals is an obstacle to marriage. If you get married, you don't have to stop traveling or saving money or working! But — and this is the thing that I think most people find to be challenging — marriage does call you into denying yourself and willing the good of the other. It calls you into love. And when you say yes to marriage, you are saying yes to this other person while saying no to your own desires. Again, this doesn't mean that you all of sudden have no desires and no needs. This does mean that you are going to practice discerning those desires within the light of matrimony.

I believe that a big reason why so many people are waiting until they are older to get married is because the narrative against self-gift begins at a very young age. If you're told a lie very early on, it's going to take much longer to reorient yourself to the truth. And there's a general fear of the vulnerability that is necessary for a true yes to marriage.

One of the questions that haunted me in my younger years was "What do you want to be when you grow up?" Sure, this seems a rather harmless question, but it's like telling a young person that who they are now has no effect on the world. The condition of "when you grow up" insists that we are unable to be anything until a certain age; and "what do you want to be" insists that right now you are nothing of worth. Or even worse — you won't be of worth until you contribute in some way. On the contrary, innate dignity is granted by mere existence. I like how Fulton Sheen said, "In each child God whispers a new secret to the world." And that secret forever changes everything.

If dignity is innate, then why is there such pressure on what a young person will be? It is because the world defines success by different standards than the Christian. The world's success is found in monetary earnings, academic degrees, the size of your house, or the newness of your car. But the success of the Christian is found in one thing: the reflection of Christ in man. So this narrative against self-gift is shrouded in careerism, fame, fortune, and worldly honor, drowning out the heart's cry to return to the Creator.

If we give into that narrative, our hearts can become cold and hard. Even as I write that, I admit that although I've rejected that narrative over and over again, it still creeps in from time to time. But, if you're reading this book, you're rejecting that lie with me, because a cold, hard heart is impenetrable. Love melts away that facade, leaving behind the alarming softness of vulnerability. That first piercing of the heart is so startling, and sometimes it downright hurts! Vulnerability feels dangerous and difficult at the beginning. Many spend their whole lives trying to overcome that fear, but the greater the risk, the greater the reward. In the end, we will find that what we risk to be loved is no risk at all, but is instead what we've been longing for our entire lives.

Your success is not found in earthly things. Your worth is not found in what you can do. And vulnerability isn't a weakness. It is a strength.

To Be Seen as We Truly Are

While you are saying no to the lies of the world, you are very much saying yes to your husband. You are saying yes to allowing him to see all the cracks and crevices of your heart (your stretch marks and makeupless face;

your struggles when life throws you curve balls) and to rejoice with you when it all works out in the end. You are saying yes to an intimacy that is simply not found outside the Sacrament of Matrimony, an intimacy that is required for conjugal life.

There's a great fear in being seen. One of my favorite scenes in the live action 2015 movie *Cinderella* is the very last scene, when she begins to descend the stairs after being locked in the attic. The words of the narrator express something we all think of ourselves: "Would who she was, who she really was, be enough? There was no magic to help her this time. This is perhaps the greatest risk that any of us will take. To be seen as we truly are."

This is the greatest risk of the matrimonial yes, and that risk can also be the greatest gift. When I said yes to marrying Jason, I was also accepting whatever vision he had of me — though not without knowing that he *loved* his vision of me, the one he saw before him, the one he envisioned for the future, and the vision he knew I am innately through *imago dei*.

Vulnerability is also a matter of trust. Can I trust this person with my heart? There's a big difference between having a desire for someone to fill your heart, a desire to be loved, and whether or not the person can do that. This is another reason why it's so important for young women to be loved as children of God before they can be loved as spouse.

Learning Belovedness

Jason and I have three daughters — Gemma (who you met briefly in the last chapter), Abigail, and Josephine. Our job as their parents is to love them well enough so as they grow older they are predisposed to recognizing what love is and what love is not. This is important for their relationship with God and their relationship with other people. When we love them well and freely, we reflect the love of the Father and teach them what it is to be a child of God. In turn, they grow in their filial identity as daughters — our daughters and daughters of the divine. Then, if the Lord calls them into spousality — whether that's through matrimony or religious life — these years will have built the foundation for them to discern how God is calling them to move forward in love.

> *When a woman does not understand her belovedness as a daughter of God, it's all too easy to be unable to recognize the voice of the Father.*

When a woman does not understand her belovedness as a daughter of God, it's all too easy to be unable to recognize the voice of the Father, to misunderstand what love looks like and how it behaves, and to be unable to recognize when that love is not true. Love Himself becomes distorted in the heart that has not been loved well. Freedom becomes entanglement. Gift becomes theft. And servanthood becomes self-serving.

Let's revisit that infamous Ephesians 5 passage again. Being subordinate to each other means that you are serving one another and on the same mission. Identity comes before mission. You cannot go out on mission if you do not know who you are. And who you are *first* is a child of God, beloved and adored by the Father.

Christ was baptized in the River Jordan, and when he rose from the waters, he heard the voice of God, "You are my beloved Son; with you I am well pleased" (Mk 1:11; Lk 3:22). Then his public ministry began. Identity and mission — this is the same route that we take within our marriage. We say yes to each other, further sharpening our identities as children and taking up our mission of becoming spouse. When those identities are realized, our marriages become beacons of hope to the world. That hope fuels the bravery needed to face a world that thinks true love doesn't exist.

Today, it takes courage to say yes and believe in the fidelity of marriage. If marriage is the greatest correlate of the nuptial relationship between Christ and the Church, and the world is losing its Christian faith, we can assume that a result will be a decrease in the number of marriages, an overall delay in people getting married, a rise in divorces, and an overall fear of lifelong commitment. The statistics reflect this deduction. "Crisis of the family" has become a buzzword in ministry around the globe, but if there is a crisis of the family then there is first a crisis of marriage, the foundation of the family.

I think we have lost the understanding that marriage is a public sacrament. Unlike the other sacraments, it is conferred by the spouses on each other. The witnesses and the priest are there to support and confirm the public declaration of marriage. When couples leave the altar and leave the Church never to return again, their marriage becomes a sort of "hiding place"* instead of a public witness, and thereby becomes a sadness felt by the entire Church. On the other hand, the couple that remains strengthens the body of Christ by their very presence. The body needs its hands and feet, its arms and legs. Each of us are the building blocks of the Church. How can Christ build his Church when the bricks for the building are invisible? They must be seen and deemed stable for use in the structure.

When couples retreat into themselves, they also retreat into their own egos. Some sacramentally married couples only return to the altar for Easter and Christmas. The Church body never gets the privilege of knowing them or being known by them. Their lives become too busy to receive the Eucharist; they become wrapped in each other, in their cares and tasks, instead of surrendering themselves each week (or each day) at the altar where their union truly began. They remain as an "I" and a "Thou" instead of a "We." And in a certain sense, the couple doesn't actually exist. The word

---

* Scola, Angelo Cardinal, *The Nuptial Mystery* (Grand Rapids, MI: Wm. B. Eerdmans Publishing, 2005), 144.

"couple" comes from the Latin word *apere* which means "to fasten." The couple that retreats into their own egos does so to either meld into each other or to remain far apart, to be separate. Neither situation allows the two to be fastened together. The couple that melds together loses individuality and the couple that remains far apart has such space between the persons that intimacy and fastening is impossible. If they remain as an "I" and a "Thou" then it becomes difficult to return to the altar where they were first made one.

The invitation extended to them at the Mass asks them to return to Christ and to become holy as Christ is holy. The vocation to marriage is the means by which the Church has invited them into this holiness. The husband and wife acknowledged this fact through their vows, said however long ago. And this isn't just an invitation to the local parish! This is an invitation to something greater, to something eternal, to the Wedding Supper of the Lamb. If they turn in on themselves, avoiding Mass and the other sacraments all together, this invitation will be so foreign that it will become uncomfortable. The Church will become a foreign land instead of a home. If the Church is not a home, then the couple won't want to serve it, won't want to join ministries or bring others into the fold. Attending Mass will become a checked box on the list of things they should do, or a box that's never checked because it's not a priority. It is a great sadness that young married couples are scarce in many parishes today.

The yes of being and becoming wife is a public declaration of good will. It is not just for you but is also for the Church. We need good marriages and we need husbands and wives who know who they are as they embark on one of the sacraments directed toward the salvation of others (see CCC 1534).

If we can reclaim the Sacrament of Matrimony and grow in our understanding of the meaning of being wife, of being spouse, then we can continue to build the Church here on earth and in the world to come.

Betrothal

What an odd word. I confess that I am saddened by the fact that we do not use this word as much anymore. Betrothal sounds so much better than engagement, doesn't it?

Engagement was first used in the early seventeenth century to signify a legal or moral obligation, a pledge. By the nineteenth century, engagement was used in the phrase "engagement ring." (In 860, Pope Nicholas I wrote to the Bulgarians answering questions concerning marriage and he mentioned rings given by the man to his bride, though he does not explicitly use the term "engagement ring.")

But *betrothal* is slightly older. The word was used as early as the fourteenth century to indicate the intent to marry. The etymology of the word is even more riveting — betrothal comes from the Middle English *be + trouthe*: to be true, to trust, to entrust.

Today, betrothal keeps its specific definition: A betrothal is "a mutual promise or contract for a future marriage." *Engagement*, on the other hand, can mean anything from a meeting, as in "I have a prior engagement"; to a military clash; to a vague "emotional involvement or commitment." Betrothal holds the dignity of marriage within its usage while engagement has broadened so much that it might not even connote marriage. The dictionary reflects the pattern that matrimony has left the sacramental life of the Church and entered into a secular world of contractual agreement.

> *When you say yes to becoming spouse, to becoming wife, you are preparing for the promise to fully entrust yourself to him. This is preparation for forever.*

When you say yes to becoming spouse, to becoming wife, you are preparing for the promise to fully entrust yourself to him. This is preparation for forever.

Today, betrothal becomes a period of haste and activity. We begin to plan and execute. We have to figure out the date for the wedding, secure the church, choose our bridal party, and make deposits. We have to say yes to the dress, pick out colors, choose save-the-date announcements and invitations, and employ calligraphers or really amazing friends to help address all the envelopes. There's so much to do.

After our Fourth of July engagement, Jason and I made plans to get married after his graduation. But when we sat down to look at the calendar, we saw his Christmas break and decided to get married that December. There was no impending reason to rush other than loving each other, and at the same time there was no feeling of hesitation to enter into the sacrament.

Now, let me pause briefly on the subject of engagement to remind you of two things. First, engagement does not equal marriage. If you are hesitant in the midst of your engagement, it is perfectly fine to pause, to lengthen the engagement for however long you need. Even if the save-the-date cards are already sent. This is forever that we are talking about here! People can change their airline tickets, but marriage is a vow of fidelity, something not as easily changed as a flight plan. It is forever (regardless of what divorce advocates may claim.) The ties of marriage, especially the Sacrament of Matrimony, cannot be cut from the heart. You are allowed to proceed at your own speed.

Second, the period of dating should be the time when you are deciding whether marriage would be appropriate for your relationship. The marriage proposal should only be a surprise because you didn't know it was going to happen *at that moment*, not because you had no idea your relationship was heading in that direction. The natural *telos* of a male-female romantic relationship is marriage. That is not a surprise. But by the time you are engaged, I hope you have really allowed your yes to be yes or your no to be no. After all, this time of preparation for the sacramental reality of marriage cannot begin without a clear decision to go toward the altar.

Back to engagement. My own betrothal period was short, only around six months, and they were filled with all the preparations to make the ceremony beautiful. But the greatest preparation during this time should occur within.

Preparing Your Heart

It's really quite appropriate that the worlds of the soon-to-be husband and wife collide quite rapidly during these months before the wedding. You will have to juggle everyone's desire for your wedding day with your own — seating arrangements, attire, venues, days, etc. But remember this: Your marriage is yours. It belongs to you and your spouse. It is to be protected, and the day of your wedding is your own as well. When you lay your head on your pillow that night, after the "I dos" and the conclusion of the reception, you begin a life together; but the preparation for that reality begins now.

Do not make the mistake of changing the plans for your wedding to cater to someone outside of you and your spouse. I'm not being too hard-nosed here! I realize there is a big difference between making sure that Aunt Sarah gets to sit with the cousin that she hasn't seen in years, and having your mother's favorite hymn incorporated into the nuptial Mass even though it makes your skin crawl. Those are different scenarios — one plausible and the other ridiculous. You and your husband have to discern those realities together and do what's best for you as a couple. These decisions will help you for years to come. This is a great time to practice charitable discussion with each other, making sure that you are listening to one another and meaning what you say. You are establishing a baseline of what to expect when making decisions together in the future. Learn now and decide well.

In Jewish tradition, the period of engagement began with the husband leaving to build their home, while the soon-to-be wife would make the other preparations for the wedding day. The husband would leave to physically prepare their home from the ground up.

You must constantly remind yourself what all the planning is for — to become gift to each other. If you miss this, your engagement will lead to frustration and empty every single plan of its ultimate meaning.

Walls and a roof do not make a home. Love establishes it. I know the temptation to give in to the flurry of activity during this time of preparation, but if the man is preparing a home and the woman is planning the ceremony, what are their interior lives directed toward? You must constantly remind yourself what all the planning is for — to become gift to each other. If you miss this, your engagement will lead to frustration and empty every single plan of its ultimate meaning. My favorite part of preparing for our wedding was planning the liturgy for the nuptial Mass. For Jason and me, our focus was servanthood. The hymns and readings that we chose all pointed toward the notion of service and sacrifice. These notions had begun to form during our engagement.

Anticipation makes all the burdens of wedding planning seem a lot lighter. I'm not a huge lover of planning. I'm horrible at it, but piecing together all the aspects of our wedding day were pure joy, simply because of my love for Jason. The love for him that manifested in my carefree approach to this planning actually became the tool which prepared my heart for marriage. Every choice was seen through the lens of my spouse. The more that we practice this other-centered decision making, the more our hearts truly open themselves up to the other to allow a special bond to be shared.

Betrothal in the Bible

There are several depictions of this time of engagement in Scripture. I'd like to focus on three of them.

The first one is in the Song of Songs. The Song of Songs is only eight chapters long and depicts the lover running about the streets in search of her beloved. Engagement at times will feel like you're running through streets looking for your beloved — amid all the tasks and plans, you'll be searching for each other. I remember asking Jason if we could go on a date and not discuss wedding plans because we had become so consumed with them that we were neglecting our connection to each other. It felt like I was searching for him though he was never really lost.

In chapter six, when the lovers finally find each other, the writer proclaims, "I am my beloved's and my beloved is mine; / he pastures his flock among the lilies" (Sg 6:3). The engagement period is a time for preparing to belong to each other — helping one another to shed egocentric eccentricities, to find each other time and time again, discovering yourself as theirs. Just prior to this verse, someone asks the woman where her lover has gone and she replies that he is in the garden, gathering lilies. In the Christian life, lilies are a symbol of resurrection, rebirth, and renewal, hence their presence on altars on Easter Sunday. This verse shows us that renewal comes from one place; and as long as you establish that place during your engagement period, you will always be able to return there. You will never lose each other when you realize that the place of rebirth is with Christ. We must always feed among the lilies.

The second scriptural reference for engagement is the Visitation. When a woman says yes to betrothal, a new seed of life is planted within her soul, a glorious expectation that begins to take root in her heart and in her mind. That joyous walk that Our Lady took to her cousin Elizabeth is part of our own betrothal. It's the result of our yes to the gift that the Holy Spirit has brought to us.

This scene always makes me laugh. I've now given birth to six children, and I cannot imagine walking any number of miles to visit anyone during any point in those pregnancies, let alone to visit a cousin that I likely haven't seen in quite some time. But the joy of engagement leads us places! Our Lady was fully involved with the life growing in her womb. She literally carried the Hope of the Nations across hillsides and fields until she came to her cousin Elizabeth.

I remember the joy of telling people that I was engaged. After Jason proposed, we spent some time going to restaurants and bars in Downtown Disney, but we both really wanted to go home and be with our friends and families. Sure, it was great celebrating this time with strangers who bought us free food and drinks in celebration — but our hearts were really longing for home. Sharing the joy of a promise like betrothal is an invitation for our friends and family to share in our hope of an enduring love.

When Mary approached Elizabeth, her cousin exclaimed:

> Blessed are you among women, and blessed is the fruit of your womb! And why is this granted to me, that the mother of my Lord should

come to me? For behold, when the voice of your greeting came to my ears, the child in my womb leaped for joy. And blessed is she who believed that there would be a fulfilment of what was spoken to her from the Lord. (Luke 1:42–45)

When we decide to enter into betrothal, we enter into Our Lady's Visitation. We greet every person with an infectious joy because the human race longs for hope in the darkness. We long to see our society believe in love that is everlasting, and when faced with true hope in the fidelity of marriage, others are inspired to hope too. An engagement with the hope of forever has the power to call others to join in rejoicing, "My soul proclaims the greatness of the Lord!"

The final scriptural reference we can explore is from the Last Supper discourses:

Let not your hearts be troubled; believe in God, believe also in me. In my Father's house are many rooms; if it were not so, would I have told you that I go to prepare a place for you? And when I go and prepare a place for you, I will come again and take you to myself, that where I am you may be also. And you know the way where I am going. (John 14:1–4)

The disciples were perplexed. Thomas even proclaimed that he didn't know the way. But the imagery that Christ uses here is no mistake. As I mentioned before, Jewish engagements meant that the groom would leave the bride to prepare their home, to physically build their house. At the Last Supper, Jesus was alluding to this reality. He leaves his beloved for this time of engagement, so that he can prepare a place for us to be with him forever.

Even though my own engagement was a mere six months, it felt like an eternity. December really couldn't come fast enough. There were times when I felt very much like Thomas, unsure of how long this period would last and whether or not the wedding day would actually ever come.

Christ responds to our longing with the same words of response that he offered to Thomas. He is the way, the truth, and the life. That is the ultimate call to task when we say yes to betrothal. We are agreeing that we can love our spouse forever, and if love is willing the good of the other, then we should be doing everything we can to introduce him to Christ and keep him as close as possible to Jesus throughout his life.

In other words, the period of engagement during which we wait for our wedding day is like the earthly state of the Church right now. The Universal Church awaits the Second Coming of Christ, with a constantly renewed hope and fidelity to the Father.

Engagement is not a time of frivolous planning or meticulous preparation, but is the very state in which we are living as members of the Body. It isn't to be taken lightly. You mustn't waste your time of waiting. Prepare your heart for the other by weeding out all the temptations and hardness. Make your heart a safe place to land. We are all, every man and woman of the Church, betrothed and waiting for the Bridegroom.

Become *engaged with* becoming more like Christ so you can invite your spouse to do the same.

New Life

The union of husband and wife unveils a new sacramental reality. In the single life, the couple stood shoulder to shoulder, facing outward at the same thing — hopefully at the Lord. And now, you stand face to face, drawn in by the gaze of your beloved and gazing at God imaged in each other. Now, your whole life is dedicated toward the vocation of marriage, helping your beloved to fully realize his own belovedness. Responding fully to this call, in tandem, will be a joyful response to your first vocation of holiness.

That response is made possible through God. It is imperative to realize that we do nothing without his grace, even the giving and receiving of the spouses one to the other through the Sacrament of Matrimony. How then does this gift and giveness integrate with our love for God? Let's turn to the *Catechism*:

> The consent by which the spouses mutually give and receive one another is sealed by God himself. From their covenant arises "an institution, confirmed by divine law,… even in the eyes of society.'"The covenant between the spouses is integrated into God's covenant with man: "Authentic married love is caught up into divine love." (1639)

Married love is caught up into divine love as a reflection of the life of God. The authenticity of such a transcendental bond cannot be denied even in the world. Catholic marriage requires a total gift of self, which is most clearly seen in the conjugal act. This act can be summed up in three words: *free, forever*, and *complete*. When each of these facets of marriage are adhered to and lived out, the appropriate result is new life.

Freedom

When you arrive at the altar on your wedding day, the first question from the presider after the liturgy of the word, will be: "Have you come here to enter into marriage without coercion, freely and wholeheartedly?"*

---

*The Order of Celebrating Matrimony, 2nd ed. (Collegeville, MN: Liturgical Press, 2016), 15.

The United States is built on the notion of freedom; but we have lost the true definition of what it is to be free. Often we think that freedom means doing whatever we want, that we find freedom in an abundance of choices and in an ability to consent or dissent without any impediment. But we have to reorient the way we understand freedom. The only true impediment to your freedom is yourself. I am always drawn back to Saint Augustine's *Confessions*, Book 8, chapter 11:

> Thus was I sick and tormented, accusing myself far more severely than was my wont, tossing and turning me in my chain till that was utterly broken, whereby I now was but slightly, but still was held. And you, O Lord, pressed upon me in my inward parts by a severe mercy, redoubling the lashes of fear and shame, lest I should again give way, and that same slender remaining tie not being broken off, it should recover strength, and enchain me the faster.

Augustine was struggling so hard against a sin that he likened it to chains. By this point, he had almost completely broken free from sin except "a slender remaining tie" that was holding him captive. I'm not sure it's even possible to be held captive by such a thing unless the will of the prisoner was weakened. His freedom was truly gone.

In order for this bond of marriage to be and remain

truly free, we must take constant and persistent steps toward breaking free from our chains. This doesn't mean that your life must be void of temptation to be truly free — temptation is part of the human experience — but it does mean that you must strive to orient your posture and actions to the will of God. His will always holds the fullness of who you are, and this is where freedom lies.

One day, I happened upon an advertisement that Fr. Jacques Phillippe* would be speaking in north Georgia the next morning. Jason and I drove all night with one baby in tow (thanks to our friends for keeping the two older children we had at that time!) to be present at this retreat.

Father Jacques said that when he arrived in the States he went to the local grocery store to get some yogurt. When he got to the dairy aisle, he was completely stunned by the number of choices. He glanced at all the labels — a variety of flavors, Greek, regular, with or without granola, different packaging, fat free, etc. Father said that this is what our worldly idea of freedom had come to: something for everyone, whatever suits one's fancy at that moment.

True freedom, on the contrary, is being shown the correct choice and having the ability to choose it. It lies before you and is not yours unless you choose the right one. Now, that can be intimidating. We often give into a sort of analysis paralysis, and end up frozen in place

---

*Fr. Jacques Philippe is a member of the Community of the Beatitudes. He is a speaker and author. One of his most well-known works is *Searching for and Maintaining Peace*. I also highly recommend *Interior Freedom* and *The School of the Holy Spirit*.

because we fear choosing the wrong thing. But do not doubt the good will of the Father. Choose and trust that he will reveal his goodness to you along the way, even if that requires you to retract a previous choice.

Every choice affects those in communion with you whether you are married or not. That's the reality of humanity. We are all utterly linked and one person's decision affects more than just the person alone. Think of Noah and the ark, Martin Luther and his theses, Mary and the baby in her womb … each is an instance of one decision that affected the world. This is the communal nature of our choices, whether they are seemingly innocuous or a turning toward sin.

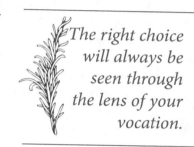

The right choice will always be seen through the lens of your vocation.

Sin, an active turning away from the love of God, separates us from the Creator and his creation. We cannot have true communion with one another when we separate ourselves from the Father. This truth, although applicable to every relationship, holds greater gravity within the sacred bond of marriage.

The right choice will always be seen through the lens of your vocation. The communal nature of man is made visible in the Sacrament of Matrimony. Perhaps before, decisions seemed isolated and contained within your own heart or space. But now, the path that lays before you will be for the good (or the bad) of your spouse and yourself. If you are truly one, all choices will now be ones that affect both of you.

Read that again: Every choice affects both of you. That's daunting! How do you avoid analysis paralysis when the task at hand seems so great? You pray for the will of the Father. You build up an interior life directed toward peace and hope in Christ. You surrender. You trust. You strengthen your spiritual life and your bond of marriage.

Frequenting the sacraments (primarily holy communion and reconciliation) provides the foundation for the strength of your marriage. It is also good practice to guard the sanctity of your bond through prayer together and apart. Praying together is imperative. Before you lay down to sleep, ask how you can pray for the other and then, with those intentions in mind, intercede with a Hail Mary or an Our Father. Pray an hour of the Liturgy of the Hours together. Offer a decade of the Rosary for each other. Even joining together for a brief morning offering and a nightly examen can do wonders for your marriage.

As you align yourself and your marriage with God's will, freedom becomes a way of a life.

When Jason or I cease to be free, we also cease to freely love each other. Our affection becomes crippled beneath the weight of sin and temptation. Seeking out the grace available from the other sacraments allows the grace in matrimony to be even more efficacious.

Fidelity

The second facet of marriage is fidelity or permanence. Since marriage is called up into divine love, the marriage bond is also called into the same fidelity that we have in covenant with God. Yet often we are tempted into forgetfulness and lack of commitment, and one cause of this is our casual approach to saying "I love you." Cardinal Angelo Scola's book *Nuptial Mystery* includes a section exploring our trite approach to those three little words. An Italian cardinal, philosopher and theologian, Scola retired in 2017 and has written extensively on theological anthropology, marriage, and the family.

Pope Benedict XVI also explained:

> Today the word "love" is so tarnished, so spoiled and so abused, that one is almost afraid to pronounce it with one's lips. And yet it is a primordial word, expression of the primordial reality; we cannot simply abandon it, we must take it up again, purify it and give to it its original splendor so that it might illuminate our life and lead it on the right path.*

Largely, we are uncomfortable with the gravity of saying "I love you" even in platonic or familial settings. If love

---

*Pope Benedict XVI, "Address of His Holiness Benedict XVI to the Participants at the Meeting Promoted by the Pontifical Council 'Cor Unum'" (address, Sala Clementina, Vatican City, January 23, 2006). https://www.vatican.va/content/benedict-xvi/en/speeches/2006/january/documents/hf_ben-xvi_spe_20060123_cor-unum.pdf

is willing the good of the other, then that good must be wielded by a subject and given to an object. With the use of technology, we've reduced a promise of fidelity to acronyms (ILY) or numeric codes (143). And when simple coding won't work we reduce the object of our love: "Love ya." The simple changing of "you" to "ya" somehow makes the expression less serious, less vulnerable and more felicitous, more egocentric. It's no longer about the object of our love but somehow about our own expression of half-hearted affection.

Even when we give in to the full form of the phrase we add equivocations as another extreme of the denial of fidelity. "I love you *so much*" and "I love you *forever*" because we've allowed the gravity of love to diminish and become so temporary that equivocation is needed. Love does not need equivocation. It's a good challenge to avoid such qualifiers.

When I first met Jason, saying "I love you" wasn't a normal part of my conversations. But after a while, after being loved by him, I was able to love more freely. Now I can tell him so, without robbing any part of the phrase of its importance.

The "I" remains as the subject of the love. This is me offering myself in vulnerability. This is me willing your good. When we do not include the I, it seems like a lack of ownership, a depossession of the act. "Love you" doesn't hold the same connotation as "I love you."

When I started saying I love you, even to members of my extended family as part of my goodbye, it was disarming. People fumble over affection, especially when it is given without condition, without an expectation of reciprocation. Marriage should be disarming. Fidelity is an expectation and a predisposition of the bond. It provides the foundation for it and continually fortifies it.

This is another reason why a constant renewal of your belovedness as a child of God is needed. A child trusts and a child expects and practices loyalty. Promises and vows are forever for a child. I'm not encouraging blind naivety, but instead the posture of receptivity instead of suspicion toward the promise of the other. When my children ask for a bowl of cereal, and I give it to them, they do not look at the bowl with suspicion. They expect that I want their good, that this bowl of cereal is exactly what they asked for, nothing more and nothing less. Because I am their mother. That relationship means that I am for them. We cannot expect failure if we maintain the life of a child.

If that expectation is not part of your understanding of marriage, then, your filial identity needs to be redeemed and reclaimed. A child expects the fidelity of the parent. I should approach my husband with a childlike belief in his love. I know that he is for me because he vowed to be with me forever. When he says, "I love you," there need not be any equivocation from him or suspicion from me.

Totality

Freedom and fidelity are nothing without the entire person. There is no freedom or fidelity if part of the person holds back. What does totality look like in the Church's eyes and in practice? Let's return to the *Catechism*:

> Conjugal love involves a totality, in which all the elements of the person enter – appeal of the body and instinct, power of feeling and affectivity, aspiration of the spirit and of will. It aims at a deeply personal unity, a unity that, beyond union in one flesh, leads to forming one heart and soul; it demands *indissolubility* and *faithfulness* in definitive mutual giving; and it is open to *fertility*. In a word it is a question of the normal characteristics of all natural conjugal love, but with a new significance which not only purifies and strengthens them, but raises them to the extent of making them the expression of specifically Christian values. (1643)

Spousal love is also total, complete. For women, two of the common impediments to this complete gift of self are shame and a lack of openness to life.

In *Love and Responsibility*, Pope John Paul II dives into what he calls the metaphysics of shame, defining it as "when something which of its very nature or in view of its purpose ought to be private passes the bounds of a person's privacy and somehow becomes public."* He goes on to say that modesty is a natural tendency. As sexual values

---

*Wojtyła, *Love and Responsibility*, 155.

are awakened in the human person, the natural tendency is to conceal — not because of their negative value, but because of their immensely positive value.

He delineates a good and a bad shame. If the only proper and adequate attitude toward the human person is love, and good shame seeks to protect the human person, then good shame must also protect the value of love itself. It conceals for the purpose of protection — for example, modesty. It is a notion of reverence; a recognition of the inexhaustible value of the human person. We are all mysteries to be discovered and these discoveries are met with the positive shame that we simultaneously desire to be known and to know one another but are also *incapable* of knowing all there is to know about one another. Shame is an invitation to love.

On the other hand, bad shame conceals the person. Like good shame, bad shame conceals but the reason for the concealment is based on lies like *I am not worthy of love, I am unlovable, I am not unique,* or *I am not enough.* And this bad shame offers an invitation not to love, but to use, which Pope John Paul II writes is the opposite of love, not hate. Without a notion of one's own goodness, one's own value and reverence, we are left with defining ourselves by what others can offer us or take from us.

Wojtyła says that this bad shame is "swallowed up by love, dissolved in it." He doesn't mean that all shame is erased by love, but that love exists *with* good shame as a natural defense against mere *use*. Shame should not diminish the value of the person but should veil that which is meant to be secret without obscuring one's innate dignity.

As a child of the nineties and learning the love of God within the evangelical Church, I was heavily involved in the True Love Waits (TLW) movement and read the book *I Kissed Dating Goodbye* more than once. The movement and the book were the pendulums of what many now know as purity culture. The True Love Waits organization promotes sexual abstinence before marriage by encouraging virginity pledges with signed contracts and even "purity rings." *I Kissed Dating Goodbye* by Joshua Harris was a *New York Times* bestseller, written by a then-twenty-three-year-old. It flew off the shelves, encouraging a new way of approaching dating through courtship and abstinence. While TLW and Harris's book shared the same Catholic view of abstinence until marriage, the approach placed so much emphasis on waiting for marriage that they wrongly reduced marriage to the conjugal act without any notion of freedom, fidelity, or totality.

There was one particularly poignant scene from Harris's book where he relays the wedding day of a fictional couple. As the couple stood at the altar, six girls got up from the congregation and began to stand in a line beside the groom. When questioned about who they were, the groom replied, "They're girls from my past."[*] Harris used this illustration to show that when a person seeks to fulfill their own desires, they ultimately use other people, and

---

[*]Joshua Harris, *I Kissed Dating Goodbye* (Colorado Springs, CO: Multnomah Books, 2003), 14.

that this self-seeking attitude has to be uprooted before one can even date. He concludes throughout the book that dating before you're ready for marriage is out of the question. Any dating prior to marriage meant that you had given pieces of yourself away, leaving the remaining fragments for your spouse. Harris advised being "whole" at all costs, avoiding intimacy for fear of vulnerability, perfecting the placid smile for fear of being too much of anything, and working hard to appear holy without any inward transformation. After all, I could sign a contract and wear a ring without any true understanding of why it was important to do so. Fake it until you make it, right?

I was seven years into my marriage and still unearthing the wounds I carried from purity culture when I picked up Wojtyła's book. I had no idea that purity culture had changed how I viewed myself, and it had nothing to do with sex.

While my husband Jason and I were dating, my mother, suffering with kidney disease, was facing another kidney failure. Jason drove me to the hospital so I could discuss next steps with her nephrologist. It was going to be a long drive, and my heart was wrecked. Yet I couldn't bring myself to show that to Jason.

Looking back, I know that I didn't want to reveal my fears to him because I was ashamed — not of my mother, not of her illness, but because I didn't want to allow him to be intimate with my pain or even intimate with my fragility. Purity culture had taught me that any crack in the porcelain — whether sexual, mental, or emotional

— was enough to be deemed unlovable. Any sort of vulnerability was contrary to the maintenance of "purity." I was ashamed of my own humanity.

Inevitably, I did tell Jason, but I made him turn around while I did so, afraid that his eyes would reveal his disdain for my vulnerability. After I blurted out what was ahead for my mother, he turned and embraced me. He walked with me through her news, and the greatest memory of that trip was driving back to our hometown with him while I wept on his shoulder. My shame was swallowed up in his love.

The profundity of shame in its proper sense — as concealment of that which is valuable, as reverence — upholds dignity. Conversely, when our value is distorted, the consequences distort our self-understanding and can damage our spiritual lives and our marriages. After all, the wholeness of the person lies in their entire being — spirit, mind, and body. When one part is negatively hidden, the whole person suffers. Marriage should be the safe space where we can be revealed. How can we be free and faithful in totality without understanding our own dignity, our own value?

Bad shame is also taught to us in some familial relationships, especially when our homes are not a place of vulnerability and comfort in every sense of the word. Home should be the place where you are able to be completely yourself. You should have the freedom to suffer, the freedom to question, the freedom to rejoice, and the freedom to lament. Many homes do not have that today because we've given in to the lie that vulnerability is a weakness when, in fact, vulnerability is a form of unification.

In fact, the Latin root for the word vulnerable is *vulnus* or wound. In the Christian life, the greatest wound is seen in the crucifixion of Christ. The wounds of Christ show us what incredible vulnerability looks like, and his wounds were a result of his unification with mankind and acceptance of all our sin. Through the self-gift of the Son, vulnerability meets and becomes intimacy. There's no intimacy without vulnerability, and that word *intimacy* comes from the Latin word *intimus* which means "inmost." Christ invites us to look at his wounds, find courage to face our own, and then to do the same within our marriages. When you allow yourself to be vulnerable, you invite your spouse into the inmost parts of yourself.

Do you remember that quote from C. S. Lewis reminding us that to love at all is to be vulnerable? I quoted the first part earlier, but read how it continues: "The alternative to tragedy, or at least to the risk of tragedy, is damnation. The only place outside Heaven where you can be perfectly safe from all the dangers and perturbations of love is Hell."* Ouch. That's a harsh reality. Vulnerability is necessary and a touchpoint of family life; without it, bad shame is introduced to the dynamic of the family. We hide ourselves because others are uncomfortable with the full vision of who we are.

After I became Catholic and we were preparing for marriage, we picked up a package from the office with

---

*Lewis, *The Four Loves*, 155.

forms and information for pre-Cana, the premarital formation process. There were customary forms, pamphlets on matrimony, and a bootlegged CD stuck between the folders. Scribbled across the front of the CD were the words "Contraception Why Not."

I listened to the CD that night and joined thousands of other Catholics in hearing this teaching of the Church in a beautiful, thoughtful talk. It was enough for Jason and me not only to accept the Church's teaching against contraception but also to champion it.

We began to practice natural family planning using the sympto-thermal method. We had no intention of avoiding pregnancy but charted my symptoms and followed our own urges. We conceived our first child after a year and a half of marriage. We had not "planned" him but we were open to receiving him as gift. Today, I have been pregnant six times. We have conceived seven children and miscarried one of them. No, my math isn't off. Our most recent pregnancy welcomed twins (Josephine and Benedict) into the world.

Yes, we have a large family, and no, it's not because our fertility awareness method failed us. In fact, if I look at my charts, I could tell you when each child was conceived and I remember us speaking about the possibility of conception each time. That's where things go awry for most couples today. This openness to life is not a discussion — instead, we view fertility as something to be fixed when it is, in fact, not broken to begin with. Your body is meant to work this way! The commitment to being open to life is part of the total gift of self. Without it, we are effectively saying to our spouse, "I trust you but not with this. You can have me but you cannot have this. You can have part of me." Giving someone half of a gift is not really a gift.

Is this always easy? Heck no. I'm not the most pleasant pregnant person, and my third pregnancy felt worse than the others. I was riding the struggle bus for most of those nine months. When Gemma was born after many, many false alarms, I was in love with her but exasperated with the possibility of being pregnant again. Without saying the words definitively, I told my husband that I was ready to contracept. I tried to manipulate Church teachings to fit my comfort level. I talked to priests and to trusted friends, and they all reiterated the stance of the Church. I scoured Google for some orthodox Catholic source that would support my desire to stop having children because it was hard. I came up empty, but was ready to do it anyway.

At the same time, I was receiving spiritual direction, and was faithful to every other Church teaching. I had not told my spiritual director about my covert operation to contracept. I remember sitting in spiritual direction, sharing about something. I cannot remember what that something was, but I do remember what my spiritual director said.

"Rachel, I don't think this situation is the heart of the problem."

I was mystified. What did he mean by "the heart of

the problem"? Of course, this thing is the problem.

"I think you're having trouble trusting God, and it isn't anything that you're sharing in this current situation. I think you even know what I'm talking about…"

I was so close to walking out of that room. I knew exactly what he was talking about, and I wanted to change the subject or tell him that he was wrong. But the Holy Spirit wouldn't let me do it. I just sat there, dumbfounded.

"Rachel, if you don't trust God with the big stuff, it's hard to trust him with the small stuff. If you let distrust fester, it will infect other areas of your relationship with him. You have to decide what you're going to do."

I really wanted to punch him in the face — a rather violent response to truth piercing the heart. Instead I walked out and went into the church to pray. And I decided to trust God— with my family size, with provisions to care for these children and the children to come, with our finances, with our home, with ministry, with work, with my marriage. I went home that night, and I told my husband that I was ready to trust. Jason was so patient with me through it all. He never pushed Church teaching on me, he didn't shove *Humanae Vitae* into my face, he didn't set ultimatums. See, the truth doesn't need defending. The truth always calls us out of ourselves, toward God. Jason didn't need to defend the truth about contraception. He just needed to pray for me to have the eyes and heart to see.

A bartender friend of mine told me that when people sit down at his bar to complain about their marriages, it's always about one of two things — money, or sex. I will tell you one secret. You are an embodied person, and what you do with your body matters so much that when your mind or heart are not all in, it will manifest itself in what you do with your body. And, if your body is doing or not doing things it should or should not be doing, those same things are at play in your heart and mind.

Do not make the mistake of thinking that what happens in your bedroom has nothing to do with your spiritual life, your mental health, your healing, or your wounds. If marriage is a call to give of yourself entirely to the other, then taking care of yourself entirely is part of taking care of your marriage.

> *Do not make the mistake of thinking that what happens in your bedroom has nothing to do with your spiritual life, your mental health, your healing, or your wounds.*

Conversations about intimacy within your marriage are difficult. I don't think there's a crash course on this in pre-Cana, and I don't think there should be. Marriage is a lifelong journey of two people getting to know each other and doing everything they can to get the other person to heaven. Part of that journey is learning to navigate this topic together.

Here are five questions that have helped us to understand our own conjugal life and that I hope will help you to deal with any fears you may feel around contraception:

1. If I want to contracept, why? This usually leads to even greater questions around fears, mistrust, and desires for control. It's an opportunity to uproot any lies that you may have been harboring within your marriage or perhaps during your lifetime.
2. How is our conjugal life and how do we practice affection outside of the bedroom? This question should come to the forefront often.
3. What are ways that we can practice intimacy when intercourse is not an option? You can Google all kinds of suggestions for this, but for us, we love a good board game, taking in a show or a movie together, going on walks hand in hand, or just enjoying a cup of tea and conversation before bed or a drink on the porch.
4. When do I feel most loved and most connected with my spouse?
5. When do I feel at rest with my spouse?

One final note on fertility awareness methods (FAM). We often talk about FAM and the hardships that come with being open to life with every act of intimacy. Yes, that part is hard; but we should also mention the difficulty of practicing chastity during fertile periods. The Lord has quite the sense of humor to create the woman so that her sexual urges are greatest during her fertile periods. How rude! "Doesn't he know that we are trying to avoid right now?" I've had that thought a few times! Yes, he does know that, and he knows you can control yourself too, no matter how much your husband looks like Keanu Reeves — or even if your kids are staying with your parents and it's the first time you've been alone at night in months! Are you open to conception right now? Are you open to expanding your family by one (or more) beautiful souls?

As you discern those questions, take note that the Church has no definitive stance on the size of one's family or even the reasons why one should or should not avoid pregnancy. In *Humanae Vitae* it says that reasons to avoid are to be "just," "serious," "well-grounded," and "acceptable." These reasons are ambiguous for our own discernment not for our confusion. Take it to prayer and discuss openly with your spouse.

One of the fruits of the Holy Spirit is self-control, and it is good practice not only to pray over your marriage but to invite the Holy Spirit into every part of it. Purity culture had taught me such disdain for intimacy and vulnerability that it took a long time for me to rightly order my understanding of the conjugal act and even affection. It is never too late to begin to have these conversations about intimacy. Every moment is a chance to begin again.

Your marriage is a source of life — for yourself and for others. Do everything you can to protect and guard it, to nourish and sustain it, and to pray for and care for it.

Forever kind of things deserve forever kind of attention.

Having biological children is not synonymous with the success of your marriage. I know many happy and holy couples that have struggled with, against and through infertility. New life means much more than having children. If you have carried the cross of miscarriage or infertility, all these pages apply to you too. You are still called to the conjugal life and all its facets — to totality, freedom, fidelity, vulnerability, and self-control. While new life may not be in the faces of biological children, that life is still reflected in other ways. Outside our family, Jason and I have been blessed with many spiritual sons and daughters, and I pray the Lord will grant us many more. The love that overflows from your marriage radiates throughout the Church and the world. The *Catechism* even says that your marriage "can radiate a fruitfulness of charity, of hospitality, and of sacrifice" (1654).

As you move forward in your vocation to marriage, new life is growing every day. My bathroom counter looks different with Jason's toothbrush. We make room in our closets and in our pantries. We make room in our hearts and sometimes, room in our wombs. Everything changes with your yes. You'll give things up. You'll learn to say no to things as your yes continues to usher in a new reality, one that's better because it's shared.

Surrender
and Trust

Pre-pandemic, Jason and I hosted a weekly gathering of young adults in our home. They filled the sunroom and we shared our faith, joy, and family with them. One night, after the meeting had ended, one of the young adults leaned over to Jason and said, "You'd be a great deacon."

I didn't listen to the remainder of that conversation, but as Jason and I were climbing into our bed a few hours later, he asked, "So do you think that's true, that I'd be a good deacon?" I laughed, "Of course, you would be, love."

Now when anyone asks Jason how he received his call to the permanent diaconate, he tells that story — except he adds this line, "When our friend said that I'd be a good deacon, I knew it was a nice idea, but it didn't become a possibility until my wife said it."

The spouse has the incredible power to take an idea and make it a possibility. While this same power is given to both husband and wife (speaking from experience here!) I believe the wife has a special ability to do this because of the natural receptivity built into her femininity. When Mary "took all these things into her heart" to ponder on them, she showed us the appropriate response to all trials, worries, opportunities, everything. We should take things into our heart first. Once there, we can take the thing, turn it over, look at it from every side, and decide if a response is needed, warranted, appropriate, and more than anything, life-giving and true.

Scripture never tells us what Mary did with all the things that she took into her heart. I have always imagined that she revisited them

> *Scripture never tells us what Mary did with all the things that she took into her heart. I have always imagined that she revisited them in prayer, laid them before the Lord, and continued receiving the Messiah even after he had left her womb.*

in prayer, laid them before the Lord, and continued receiving the Messiah even after he had left her womb. This
receiving was growing in knowledge of who he is as her
Son and as the Messiah of the world.

As you grow in your marriage and spousality, you
will learn more and more about the other person, and it
is best to follow Mary's suit. You can tuck away gift ideas
when your spouse likes a post on social media, or you
can take note of how well he handles parenthood or a
work situation so you can bring it up when he needs that
extra pep one day. (It's always good to bring those com-
pliments up, the moment you think of them *and* later!
Both/and!) When you take something into your heart
and give it back to your husband later through gift or
words of encouragement, you give his dignity back to
him, you remind him of how loved he is; and I firmly
believe that our ability to do this for one another helps
us to continue to learn about who we are. Pope St. John
Paul II pointed out in *Mulieris Dignitatem* that women
have a special ability to pay attention to another person:

> It is commonly thought that *women* are more
> capable than men of paying attention *to another
> person,* and that motherhood develops this pre-
> disposition even more. The man — even with
> all his sharing in parenthood — always remains
> 'outside' the process of pregnancy and the baby's
> birth; in many ways he has to *learn* his own *'fa-
> therhood' from the mother.*" (no. 18)

What he says about the sharing of parenthood is true, but the same is also true about the sharing of spousality. You will learn about your call to be wife, and your husband will learn about his call to be husband, by watching, learning, and answering to the needs of the other person and affirming and calling out their charisms and gifts. At times, your husband may remain outside of who he is without your ability to learn who he is and to share that learning with him. What needs does your husband have that you have a particular gift for fulfilling? What gifts does your husband have that require your affirmation in order for him to gain confidence and belief in that gift?

Cooperate and Participate

With each pregnancy, my sense of smell rises and my energy plummets. The first time I was pregnant, I remember taking the test and staring at the two little lines in disbelief. We were as ready as we could be, but I was still taken aback by the wonder of it all. When Jason got home from work, I told him what I had found out.

"I think we're pregnant."

"You *think* we're pregnant?"

"Yes. I guess I'm not sure how these things work. I've never done this before! Should we take another test?"

We took three more tests, and the two little lines appeared each time. I was a mother with that first positive test, and I became more and more a mother with each of those tests and every day after that. And Jason was a dad with that first test, too, but he didn't know it yet. That's what Pope St. John Paul II means when he says "[The man] has to learn his own fatherhood from the mother."

This truth is not just for fatherhood. It's for other areas of our lives too. For instance, it was true for Jason's call to the diaconate. When he asked if I thought he'd be a good deacon, I knew the answer without question. I had already seen him serve others in every area of his life. Why not sacramentalize that reality through holy orders?

I had spent so much time praying for Jason as spouse and father that when the diaconate calling was before us, it became a natural echo of who he is. I didn't have to think about it. I didn't need to take it to prayer. In that second, I knew that if it were his calling, he would be an excellent deacon. I had contemplated, and in speaking the fruit of that contemplation, I cooperated.

This contemplative cooperation is also seen in the life of Mary. All young Jewish women knew about the prophecies of the Messiah, and they all knew that one of them would be called to carry the Messiah in their womb. Mary had contemplated this all her life, so, of course, her response to Gabriel was without hesitancy. She chose to cooperate with that which she had spent her whole life carrying in her heart. At the Annunciation, the Blessed Mother offers this beautiful prayer for all mankind to echo, "Let it be to me according to your word" (Lk 1:38).

Let it be to me. May I have the freedom to participate with God's will, with God's Holy Spirit.

The Holy Spirit descended upon her womb and the Incarnation occurred. God became flesh and dwelt among us. Mary is called the *spouse* of the Holy Spirit and her docility shows us a brilliant and often overlooked aspect of spousality — cooperation with the Trinity to allow an incarnational reality for the other person. If Jason's diaconate calling was a natural echo of who Jason is, I couldn't hear it without making contemplative cooperation a habit of our marriage. And when that cooperation left my mind and heart and was voiced to him, I began to participate in what had already been revealed.

Let's look at another example of cooperation and participation. When I was in fifth grade, my teacher did these end-of-the-year predictions for us. She made certificates that included her prediction of what we would be doing one day. She predicted that in fifteen years I would be an editor of a large newspaper. The next line said, "I'm making this prediction because you write so well." I think that simple certificate incarnated a reality for me. Fifteen years later, I wasn't an editor of a large newspaper — but I was working my way through college to work in that field. Today, that affirmation of my writing is an echo of the calling that my fifth grade teacher shared with me many moons ago, and it's echoed so loudly that many doors have opened to use this gift, including the door to write this book.

The beauty of the Incarnation is that it is not something out of nothing. It is making flesh — or making real — something that already exists. Just as our children were born from our love, Jason's diaconate was born out of the seed of service already growing in his heart.

When something is created, it is never created in isolation or meant to be turned in on itself. Once something is incarnated, there must be a willingness to give it away.

Imagine walking into a friend's house and finding a bunch of incredible artwork. Intricate and beautiful canvas paintings line the walls. So you ask your friend, "Who's the artist?" And they reply, "Me." I think I'd feel a bit betrayed and would go down the rabbit hole asking, "Do I even know who you are?!" Because to create something beautiful and then to keep it all to yourself seems selfish and even a bit ridiculous.

The only thing that has been created for itself is man. But, even then, as *Gaudium et Spes* so aptly puts it, in order for man to find himself he must make a sincere gift of himself. You do not find out who you are until you give yourself away.

We work every day to raise our children not only as responsible citizens, but more than that, as saints. We nurture them and help them grow for the sole purpose of ushering them into the world, so they can share whatever they have gleaned in their lives from their own ability to be loved. Ultimately, we give them back to Christ. But how does this apply to being a spouse?

The moment you say yes to being his wife, you also

say yes to letting him go.

There will be missions that need your husband, things that he will need to do and people he will be called to serve. But he cannot do this fully without your support and prayers. Within the Sacrament of Matrimony, the Lord will never ask you to do something that violates or harms your vocation. If marriage is a conduit of grace and nature builds on grace, then it is safe to assume that any calling received after marriage will build upon the very foundations of that sacrament.

For us, this reality became evident during formation for the permanent diaconate. As we inched closer to ordination, it became more and more real that Jason would soon be serving the Church in a very visible way, on the altar. Seeing him in an alb was one thing, but a dear friend of ours gave him a dalmatic for his birthday before his ordination. He threw it on and was struck with joy. I sat across from him in absolute awe, choking back tears. Here he was, this husband of mine standing across from me, his bride, wearing the garment that calls him to the altar to serve the Bride the Church, which also happens to include me too. It was an overflow of grace from his identity as husband to his joining with the Bridegroom in service to the Bride.

A few months prior to this, I was praying the rosary while driving to our monthly diaconate formation retreat, and I came to the second Luminous Mystery, the wedding at Cana. In my mind, I was walking through the wedding reception, amid the joy and laughter; and then, I saw that the wine vessels were empty. I imagined that the Blessed Mother was filled with sadness and joy at that moment. "The vessels are empty but my Son can fix this. I can ask him to make wine but the moment I do will be the moment that he has to leave me."

Mary's fiat was the beginning of a perpetual consent to surrender. Yes, I will be the mother of God only to let him grow and leave me one day. Yes, I will allow a sword to pierce my heart in service of the suffering to come. Yes, I will ask him to help with the wine just so that his public ministry will begin. Yes, I will follow him even if it means following him to his death.

We can each answer individual calls and, through mutual prayers and faith in one another, we are able to support one another's ministries, one another's gifts and callings, because they are actually an expression of our love.

When either the husband's or the wife's gifts and ministries are a threat to the other, it is because the spouse's approach to marriage is insecure. The sacrament itself is sealed by God and cannot be dissolved (see CCC 1640). Since we believe that to be true, then we must recognize that if a marriage feels unstable, it is because of the lack of sure footing for either or both spouses. But if both husband and wife are secure within this covenant, then they can allow it to grow to its fullest potential — which will always be something that is rooted in love for each other and then grows out to create life, perhaps through children but always through love that extends out into the world. In order for that growth to happen, we have to be okay with letting go. You cannot grow something beautiful if you choke the life out of its stems.

The Church has one goal in mind for life here on earth: union with God. This is true for us as individuals and especially true for spouses who most resemble the covenant between Christ and the Church. So when we marry, that initial yes which includes "till death do us part" is a declaration written on our mortality. We let each other go as we surrender them to the Lord through ministry or gift of talents, but the ultimate call to letting a spouse go is through death. The ancient practice of *memento mori* ("Remember your death") meets marriage in this way. If we habitually remember our death, then we learn that all our time here on earth is preparation for eternity. This includes the preparation made within marriage — through and for the love of our spouse.

An Act of Trust

When Mary invited Christ to begin his public ministry at the wedding at Cana, her ability to make that invitation wholeheartedly was because her eyes were fixed on God, not her son. So it must be with your husband.

There are times within my own marriage when I worry that I am not detached enough, when I am reminded that I need to grow in trust.

One night, Jason was coming off a jam-packed week of work, filled with late nights and high stress, and topped off with an 18-mile overnight hike with friends. He was spent! That night, he went to bed without so much as a good night. As I was cleaning the house after everyone was in bed, a chore that we usually share, there was a brief moment when I was tempted to grow bitter toward him. All these thoughts ran through my mind: *He shouldn't have gone on that hiking trip. He couldn't even say good night to me! I really wish he had been more present with us tonight.*

And while there were truths amid the growing bitterness, it all boiled down to one lie hidden beneath all my angst: He must not really love me.

What an obnoxious lie. See, this same man had also texted me right before he entered the woods for his hike. "Thank you so much for letting me do this. Love

> *I trust him. I take him at his word. I cherish when those words become action. I believe what he promised me. I am his wife.*

you so much I can hardly stand it." And as he was coming home from his hike, I was on my way to a hotel room that he had booked for me so I could have time away to write this book!

But there I was straightening pillows on the couch and hearing the all too familiar lie that my marriage must be a sham. Have you experienced this doubt or something similar? How do we overcome this?

Trust.

I trust him. I take him at his word. I cherish when those words become action. I believe what he promised me. I am his wife.

This trust only arises from the trust that I have in my relationship with God. I also trust him. I take him at his word. His word became action in the person of Christ. I believe what he promised me. He made me Jason's wife.

We receive these truths and ponder them in our hearts. That pondering is like resting in the love from our husband. We do not need a constant declaration of his love. Instead, we need to learn that his love is true and that the declaration we seek is found in his vow, his choosing to enter into this sacrament with us. And when we believe that vow, it becomes a passive reception of his love that is called into action every day. I believe he loves me, so I will make his breakfast. I believe he loves me, so I carry him in prayer. I believe he loves me, so I will remind him of that appointment he has today. I believe he loves me. End of sentence. Period. Our trust produces peace.

Healing

At first, I didn't think marriage was in the cards for me. I was born out of wedlock, adopted by missionaries, and brought to the other side of the world. Later, my adoptive parents got divorced and remarried. My brothers (also through adoption) have each been married and divorced twice. Broken marriages were all around me. I just didn't believe that a forever kind of love could exist, and I viewed the world through the pain that had become my reality.

Do not misread those sentences as someone who didn't feel called to marriage. I simply didn't believe in the *possibility* of marriage. I knew the definition — unity of man and woman, reciprocal love and servanthood, fidelity — but I had not seen it. I didn't believe in the thing itself, and so my understanding was fractured. I could not enter fully into my vocation until my vision, my way of seeing, was healed.

Within the Sacrament of Matrimony, the man and the woman take part in a beautiful dance. We learn the facets of each other's hearts and the ways in which he receives love most effectively. We learn to speak in a language that our beloved can understand. It's not a language built upon only on the understanding of his personality, but it is also grounded in his human formation, his upbringing, the way that he experienced love, and also how healing has pieced together what may have been a fractured view.

Within ourselves, we must give and receive a certain healing; and there is also a healing that each spouse offers to the other.

Seeking Healing for Yourself

At Disney World, there's a place in Epcot's Mexico Pavilion where you can watch a glassblower at work. The art of glassblowing is entrancing — the light from the flame, the intricacy of reworking the heated glass into other shapes with tweezer-like tools, and the breath from the glassblower passing through a straw-like blowpipe forming bubbles in the glass that can easily be molded and changed.

It's quite similar to a potter creating with clay,

though there's an important difference between the glass smith and the potter. As I watched the glassblower, he made the occasional mistake. He'd bend the glass a little too far or the end would taper too broadly; and he would throw that piece into a pile of forgotten, misshapen pieces of glass. But the potter, when he makes a mistake, handles things a little differently. Listen to the way the potter works with the clay in this account from the Prophet Jeremiah: "And the vessel he was making of clay was spoiled in the potter's hand, and he reworked it into another vessel, as it seemed good to the potter to do (Jer 18:4). The clay is not discarded but instead is reworked into something new.

Saint Athanasius goes even deeper with this idea in his work *On the Incarnation*:

> A portrait once effaced must be restored from the original. Thus the Son of the Father came to seek, save, and regenerate. No other way was possible. Blinded himself, man could not see to heal. The witness of creation had failed to preserve him, and could not bring him back. The Word alone could do so. But how? Only by revealing himself as man. For as, when the likeness painted on a panel has been effaced by stains from without, he whose likeness it is must needs come once more to enable the portrait to be renewed on the same wood: for, for the sake of his picture, even the mere wood on which it

is painted is not thrown away, but the outline is
renewed upon it.

Being renewed as *imago dei* is the goal of healing. Notice
I didn't stay "renewing yourself." You must allow yourself
to be renewed. You must be clay in the potter's hands or
the canvas on the painter's easel — docile, surrendered,
willing to be made whole. Healing is constantly being
offered by God, and to be whole, we must accept and
participate in it.

Christ became man. The Word was made flesh in
order to redeem the very language and vision of love.
Man had come to view himself as sinful, unforgivable,
beyond repair; and Christ came to remind man that we
are not too far to be reached. Further, our humanity was
and still is the means for God to communicate himself
to the world. Christ became man so that man could see
that he is like God. Your skin, your flesh, your humanity,
your existence is not bad. You are good.

Say that to yourself: I am good. I am made in the
image and likeness of God, and I am good.

This is the healing that we must receive from God
for ourselves, believing in our own innate goodness.
You were created by Goodness himself, meant for love,
meant for more. This is the first step to repairing our
broken view and healing the wounds that are revealed.
When you realize that your existence is good — that you
don't need to do anything to earn it or even have the
ability to change that truth — then you can rest in your

striving and receive the divine inspiration to be actively good. Take a breath (the root word of *inspiration* is inspire, to breathe) and by that very breath, you are good. Go and do good too.

Put On Your Own Oxygen Mask First

Healing must begin independently from your spouse because you are not meant to count on your spouse for healing. To return to who we are meant to be, our tarnished image is not to be restored in the likeness of our spouse but in the likeness of God. To seek restoration in the image of your husband is not only unfair to you but is unfair to him.

Your husband cannot be your source for refilling your tank. If you and your spouse only draw from each other — praying together, working only on your spiritual life together — you'll inevitably run dry because there's no place to fill up. You'll grow resentful of him because he cannot be all that you are expecting him to be. How do you fill the tank from its true source? Personal prayer and devotions. Take time alone to pray. Go by yourself to adoration. Take up personal devotions and resolve to do them alone while lifting up your spouse.

There are other ways beyond personal prayer to help you continue your personal healing. Develop holy friendships with like-minded people. Speak with a therapist. Receive the healing being offered to you. When your individual healing is underway, it then allows the space for you to share that healing with your spouse and for you to offer healing to each other. You cannot give to someone something that you do not have!

On an airplane, we're always given the preflight safety presentation. We're reminded that if there is extreme turbulence or an emergency, breathing masks will drop out of the ceiling. And the announcer says, "Secure your own mask before helping others." On the battlefield, it is the unwounded or the bandaged soldier who goes into the frontlines to help the wounded. The soldier or field medic cannot stop someone from bleeding if he himself is hemorrhaging at the same time. The soldier must be of good health, or at least healthier than the wounded, to offer any real assistance.

It's prideful to think that you somehow are superhuman, not requiring a moment of silence or a break to collect yourself. Avoiding self-care is a form of dehumanization.

Both on the airplane and in the field, we are reminded that care for oneself enables us to care for others. Make time for yourself. Whether that's picking up a good book, going for a walk, taking a long bath or hitting the gym, you must be intentional about caring for your mind, body, and soul. When do you feel most at rest? When do you find it easiest to pray? Visit those places as a good starting point to opportunities for self-care.

Self-care is not a selfish act. It's not selfish to need a moment to recharge. It *is* selfish to avoid the recollection for fear of appearing needy. It's prideful to think that you somehow are superhuman, not requiring a moment of silence or a break to collect yourself. Avoiding self-care is a form of dehumanization.

You Can't Heal by Hurting

A friend of mine was going through a sloppy divorce after both he and his wife were unfaithful. I asked him why he cheated, and he said that he couldn't stand that his ex-wife wielded so much power over him. He said he knew there was the possibility of her rolling over in bed one morning to exclaim that she no longer loved him. He didn't like the possibility of that kind of pain, so he decided to hurt her before she could hurt him.

What a sad plan. My friend had given into the lie that in order to be healed, suffering must be avoided. On the contrary, you cannot heal yourself through someone else's pain — and love requires suffering.

Saint Ambrose said, "One cannot heal himself by wounding another." This is one of my favorite quotes, because it offers a gentle reminder that our healing is found in our wholeness and by affirming the wholeness of others. Our human nature is built for community, so when one member of the body suffers, we all suffer. If one of us is wounded, we are all wounded together.

I previously mentioned the C. S. Lewis quote that begins, "To love at all is to be vulnerable." But I didn't tell you that the first time I read it, I felt like someone knocked the air out of me. I'm sure that I audibly and exasperatedly said, "Well, I want no part of it then!" — until I found out that to love is to give. And when I truly give, when I truly become vulnerable, arms out and ready for whatever may come, then I am truly able to become and to see glimpses of who I am really made to be. Loving this way is not an easy task. It's painful to pry your own ego out of your hands and to push your chin into the air so you can look beyond yourself at the person that you love. But this hurt reminds us that love is real; in the words of St. Teresa of Calcutta, "Love to be real, it must cost — it must hurt — it must empty us of self."

Healing Together

When Jason and I got married, we began a journey of healing together, one that coincides with our ongoing individual journeys of healing. Now remember, when I say healing, I speak of a returning to *imago dei,* a return to a belief that we are innately good, that I am not the sum of my weaknesses and failures but I am the sum of the Father's love for me and my real capacity to become the image of his Son.* As spouses, we can provide that for each other and be conduits of the Lord's healing, too.

The marital bond creates an intimacy that is so grave that we are able to remind each other of who we

---

*Pope St. John Paul II, "Apostolic Visit to Toronto, 17th World Youth Day Solemn Mass, Homily of the Holy Father John Paul II," (homily, Downsview Park, Toronto, July 28, 2002).

are called to be and who we really are. The sacramental grace is not limited to the marriage rite — meaning the grace doesn't stop flowing when the wedding is over. In fact, it is safe to assume that the more that spouses are able to help restore *imago dei* in each other, the more the grace of their sacramental union continues to flow. Grace flows according to one's predisposition to give and receive it. Think of it like this. Water flows naturally down a stream, but rocks and fallen debris can cause impediments to that flow of water; detritus can slow it down or, if there's enough, stop it all together. First and foremost, grace is a gift from God. We do not give grace to one another, but our decision to receive healing, to remove the rocks and the branches that have kept the grace from flowing, allows us to participate with the flow of the river, or the flow of grace that is always being offered to us.

The healing doesn't have to end on our wedding day; we don't have to be perfect in order to become spouse.

The healing doesn't have to end on our wedding day; we don't have to be perfect in order to become spouse. The healing can be ongoing, perpetual, as long as the spouses are willing to continually do the work to tap into the grace that God offers. This requires not only individual work but also laboring together.

In our home, we have the gift of an extra room that

is built into our garage. It served as an office space for the previous owners, and contained a desk, a filing cabinet, and harsh maroon carpet. The space was vacant for a very long time until one year I decided to change it as a gift for Father's Day. I ripped up the carpet, painted the walls, and had hard wood floors installed. I purchased a beautiful crucifix and a kneeler, turning the space into a prayer room. It is now an oasis for each of us, for us together, and for our children. Tears have been shed in that room. Hearts have been restored. Mass has been celebrated. Life has been renewed.

The prayer room is a space for authentic love, radical self-gift through prayer. Within that space I can lay all that I am at the feet of Christ, kneel before his cross and allow myself to be healed. When I do that, and when Jason does that, we are then able to extend our own healing to each other and, in turn, to our children.

The self-gift that we are called to in matrimony not only mirrors the Trinitarian life of God, but it also beckons us to recall the Paschal Mystery. To truly bring about healing, there must be suffering and death. To be resurrected, the body has to enter the tomb. Often, we want the Resurrection, but without the trials of the Triduum, especially the final breath of Good Friday. Yet death is inevitable, both physically and figuratively, and we are invited to live every moment within that awareness.

I once asked Jason, who works in orthopedic surgery, what happens if someone breaks his arm and allows it to heal without treatment or resetting the bone.

"Would the bone heal?"

"Yes. But if it hasn't been reset, it will heal incorrectly. The person might even be able to use his arm but he won't be able to use it the way that it was intended to be used."

"What if he wants it to be fixed after it has healed incorrectly?"

"Then, he has to come in and see us, and we have to rebreak it in order to fix it."

I was astounded. So many of us, even within our own marriages, have settled for a "healed incorrectly" version of ourselves. We are wounded and broken, but we seek to ignore what has happened, or we aren't equipped to seek restoration. We move on, and now we walk around crippled, attempting to love with a broken heart.

If we are attentive to the movements of our hearts, we can quickly identify where and what wounds we may carry. When someone approaches a physical wound, we naturally flinch or guard the wound. Spiritual wounds or the wounds in our hearts are protected in the same way. The following questions may help you uncover wounds that you may not be aware of:

- Is there a subject that you cannot broach with your husband?
- Is there an event or a memory that causes you to flinch when you think about it?
- When you become defensive or are hurtful toward your husband, what are the circum-

stances that cause such a response?

The good news is this. You are functioning. You are loving. You are being loved. But there is an even greater reality that awaits you if you decide to receive the healing that Christ offers us. It will require a rebreaking, a revisiting of the wound, a resetting of the bone. That will hurt. But the promise of the grave is the resurrection. You can be made whole. You are intended to love and be loved as your whole self. There is more than functioning within woundedness, for you and for your spouse. There is healing. There is joy. There is wholeness.

We allow our own healing to provide healing for others. If we do not, we only transfer our own pain. It is far better to share our own wholeness, thereby helping one another to be whole again too.

Evangelization

One of my favorite movies, *The Notebook*, opens with a monologue from actor James Garner as the character Duke, who is getting through his life in a nursing home. He approaches a woman in the nursing home to read to her, even after the nurse says that the woman may not be up for it on that day. Duke continues reading to her the love story of Noah and Allie, how they met, how they fell in love, and how their story played out. The film is quite enrapturing, but one thing that has always stuck out to me is how contagious the love story was. The nursing home staff become as much a part of the story as they are listeners.

Love by its very nature is self-surrender. When surrendered, the self becomes other-focused and that focus, in turn, draws the object of focus out of himself. Love is a self-surrender that inspires others to self-surrender. If evangelization is sharing the good news, then the good news of a love that is truly for the other is indeed worth sharing.

Scriptural Signposts

The marriage covenant serves as a reflection of the covenant between Christ and the Church, and there are touchstones within the life of Christ that serve as signposts for the Sacrament of Matrimony.

Christ became man within the context of a man's and a woman's promises to marry. In Jewish tradition, Joseph and Mary were already on their way to being married. Joseph was in the process of preparing their home as Mary prepared herself for their nuptial vows. It was within the context of betrothal that the Annunciation occurred, that Mary gave her fiat, and that the hope of the world was conceived. This is why proposals and engagements are causes for celebration. While engagements aren't permanent in themselves, we celebrate because something is happening. The soon-to-be husband and wife are moving toward forever together. The engagement points toward the marriage vow. When the man and woman become husband and wife, the great call of altruistic love is realized, and contains within its possible fecundity the ability to create new life.

Joseph and Mary were then called to live out a life of radical self-denial. Their entire lives were focused on raising the Son of God, raising the one who would redeem the world. When the angel Gabriel invited them into the salvation story, he invited them separately. They responded separately and then responded together. They chose to lay down their lives for one another and for Christ — and look at the fruit that their response has given to all of us! When we respond to this invitation of self-denial, it proliferates.

In a world that speaks only the language of selfishness, the self-denial we choose every day in the Sacrament of Matrimony speaks volumes.

Mary and Joseph's courage to deny self continues to inspire couples today to respond to a call of love that transcends our selfish desires. While this might not look like the same self-denial that Mary practiced, the transcendence is still there. It might look like waking up a little bit earlier to cook breakfast for my husband. It may be carrying the responsibilities of the household alone for a few days so that he can go on retreat. It may look like taking the trash out if he's working late (my least favorite chore). It may look like sitting by his bedside when he's ill. It may look like visiting his grave when he has passed away. In a world that speaks only the language of selfishness, the self-denial we choose every day in the Sacrament of Matrimony speaks volumes.

The Nativity took place in a stable with hay, animals, and a feeding trough as a baby crib. But this was such a great moment of evangelization — shepherds and wise men came from afar to hear, see, and touch the good news. The birth of the Christ-child within Joseph and Mary's sacramental marriage drew other people into the story of redemption.

Marriage plays a fundamental role in the life of Christ and remains so after his death and resurrection. His first miracle took place at a wedding (see Jn 2), and during his public ministry, the people asked him about marriage and divorce (Mt 19 and Mk 10). This questioning on marriage and divorce was so significant that it was included in two Gospels. After Christ's death, Saint Paul expounds on marriage (Eph 5), and in Revelation, we hear about the "wedding supper of the Lamb" (19:9).

A Wedding Is Evangelization

At a friend's wedding, Jason and I were on the dance floor for a slow song, wrapped in each other's arms and swaying to the music. Our daughter Abigail, about three years old at the time, walked up to me and tugged on my dress. When I looked down she extended her arms to me, demanding, "Hold me!"

I picked her up and for the rest of that song, she was wrapped in my and Jason's arms. As we swayed to the music, she swayed with us. When we returned to the table, another friend grabbed his phone and showed me a photo he had snapped of us on the dance floor with Abigail. He said, "We all sat here and watched you guys. It's like the Trinity."

Seeing two people not only passionately in love but also passionately choosing to love is contagious. It's like being on a busy street and seeing a group of people looking into the sky. You'd want to look into the sky too. What are they all looking at? I want to look at it too!

The wedding should be the beginning point for this evangelization. The *Catechism* states this by calling marriage a liturgical act, an ecclesial order, a state of life, which draws on the public character of consent. Here's exactly what the *Catechism* says:

> This is the reason why the Church normally requires that the faithful contract marriage according to the ecclesiastical form. Several reasons converge to explain this requirement:
>
> - Sacramental marriage is a liturgical act. It is therefore appropriate that it should be celebrated in the public liturgy of the Church;
> - Marriage introduces one into an ecclesial order, and creates rights and duties in the Church between the spouses and towards their children;
> - Since marriage is a state of life in the Church,

> certainty about it is necessary (hence the obligation to have witnesses);
> - The public character of the consent protects the "I do" once given and helps the spouses remain faithful to it. (1631)

There's a lot packed into this quote. Liturgical acts are to be performed in public, and the public nature of the Sacrament of Matrimony is a constant point of renewed fidelity for the spouses, too. Any public consent always has a stronger gravitational pull than a private promise. "Marriage introduces one into an ecclesial order" means that this sacrament draws each spouse into closer relationship with the Church — ecclesial — and each other, forming the governing body of the family and all humanity — order (see CCC 1537). As husband and wife, we renew ourselves and then are able to provide that renewal, that sense of self, for others. Marriages that become grounds of renewal for the spouses also provide this renewal to those around them.

In fact, there's such a call to evangelization within marriage that the *Catechism* calls this sacrament one at the service of communion:

> Two other sacraments, Holy Orders and Matrimony, are directed towards the salvation of others; if they contribute as well to personal salvation, it is through service to others that they do so. They confer a particular mission in the

Church and serve to build up the People of God.
(1534)

By accepting your place in this ecclesial order, within
your marriage, you contribute to your personal salvation by service to others, first to your spouse and then
to others. Your marriage has the capacity to join in the
mission of the Church to build up the People of God
and to serve them.

Giving the Gift of Joy

The joy that is manifested
in the hope of a good marriage grants permission for
other people to believe in
marriage again. As you decide to fully live out your
call to marriage, the sacrament continues to be re-
newed, allowing the spirit
to move within and out
into the world through it,
bringing about sanctifica-
tion for yourselves and for
the whole world. All for the
glory of God!

*Your marriage has
the capacity
to join in the
mission of
the Church
to build up
the People of
God and to
serve them.*

If you don't believe me, check out what *Gaudium et
Spes* has to say:

> By virtue of this sacrament, as spouses ful-
> fil their conjugal and family obligation, they
> are penetrated with the spirit of Christ, which
> suffuses their whole lives with faith, hope, and
> charity. Thus they increasingly advance the
> perfection of their own personalities, as well as
> their mutual sanctification, and hence contrib-
> ute jointly to the glory of God. (no. 48)

Maintaining a joyful, holy, sacramental marriage is
proof of the love of God. Seeing a husband and wife truly love each other is magnetic and mesmerizing. You can
barely take your eyes off them, and you want to know all
the secrets of their loving relationship. It's more prized
than the highest riches. In fact, a joyful, holy, sacramental marriage can change the way society views marriage,
from a union destined for divorce, to one that is destined for life and hope. How can this be, unless we are
beacons of hope ourselves and we raise children who are
rooted in this hope?

Gaudium et Spes continues:

> Authentic conjugal love will be more highly
> prized, and wholesome public opinion created
> about it if Christian couples give outstanding
> witness to faithfulness and harmony in their
> love, and to their concern for educating their
> children also, if they do their part in bringing
> about the needed cultural, psychological and

social renewal on behalf of marriage and the family. Especially in the heart of their own families, young people should be aptly and seasonably instructed in the dignity, duty and work of married love. Trained thus in the cultivation of chastity, they will be able at a suitable age to enter a marriage of their own after an honorable courtship. (no. 49)

Every so often, I ask our kids what vocation they think they might be called to. Jeremiah, our ten-year-old, was waking up one morning, groggily lying on the couch, when I asked him about his vocation. He said that if he had to decide today, he would want to be married because he would "have a wife and get to be a dad." One could surmise that he admires that Christian state of life because he has seen it lived well. At least, that is my prayer.

If we accept the betrothed state of Christian people waiting on the second return of Christ, then we are part of the Bride as we wait and prepare for the Groom. If we accept our call to marriage as a reflection of the Trinity of God, then we are part of the perpetual self-gift. If we truly understand this notion of self-gift, then we also realize that as we give of ourselves, we are healed and we become more ourselves. We become truly free through our own healing by self-gift. And when a husband and a wife are truly free, they become childlike. There's an innocence required when you entrust yourself into the care of another. Thus, becoming child is really the foundation for becoming spouse.

8

Becoming Wife

Being a spouse is not only a state of life, but also a daily task. While we are wives, we also continually learn how to practice more and more being a wife, being a spouse. We grow in support of our husband. We learn how to meet each other's needs. We call out the good that we see and invite him to remember his true identity as a child of God. That premiere identity is the basis for our shared spousality. In order for me to be and become wife, I must continue to become a child.

In Matthew 18:1–5, we read:

At that time the disciples came to Jesus saying,

"Who is the greatest in the kingdom of heaven?" And calling to him a child, he put him in the midst of them, and said, "Truly, I say to you, unless you turn and become like children, you will never enter the kingdom of heaven. Whoever humbles himself like this child, he is the greatest in the kingdom of heaven. Whoever receives one such child in my name receives me."

Innocence is unaware of the temptations of the world, but virtue withstands the temptations of the world and moves forward with hope.

If you ask any of my children, you'll find they are in quite the rush to grow up. I remember being in that same rush, wanting to truly be "free" — which I thought was the opposite of being restricted to the rules and regulations imposed on me by my parents. I tell my children to slow down, don't rush, that one day they'll miss the days of their childhood

In Christ's exhortation, we are asked to do more than just begin life as little children — something out of our control and beyond our will — but to end life like that too. Childhood is fleeting but can be found again and again, and even as we grow older we must at the same time grow younger. We tend to think that childlikeness must mean innocence, which some confuse with ignorance or naivety. But childlikeness is not easily maintained in a world like ours. Innocence is unaware of the temptations of the world, but virtue withstands the temptations of the world and moves forward with hope. I think you see this in the greatest saints — adults with childlike faces, like St. Thérèse of Lisieux and Servant of God Thea Bowman. Thérèse felt like God was absent from her toward the end of her life, but never ceased serving him. Thea Bowman was not ignorant of the need for peace and especially racial reconciliation, but she continued to evangelize with joy. Both women faced the wiles of the world and looked forward in hope, leaving them with childlike faces and childlike joy. They were adults who cultivated their childlike hearts. As a spouse, you are also called to reclaim your childlikeness.

Hans Urs von Balthasar, a Swiss theologian who was a close friend of the late Pope Benedict XVI, noted that an adult who desires to live with childlike faith must have the following traits: a sense of wonder and amazement, an attitude of thanksgiving, an appreciation for mystery, and the ability to take time as it comes. He outlined these traits in his short work *Unless You Become Like This Child*. Let's explore these four traits through von Balthasar's writing, and bring these thoughts into our journey of becoming wife.

Wonder and Amazement

*"We can be sure that the human Child
Jesus was in amazement over everything:
beginning with the existence of his loving
Mother, then passing on to his own existence,
finally going from both to all forms offered
by the surrounding world, from the
tiniest flower to the boundless skies."*

Fireworks, ocean waves, mountain vistas, a running river, falling snow, lightning bugs in a vacant field on a dark night — these are just a few of the things that spark wonder and amazement. But there's so much wonder to be found even within the human person: a woman with child, the first time a baby smiles, toddlers learning to walk.

For the wife, there's a certain sense of wonder and amazement both when you slide the engagement ring on your finger, and when you "say yes to the dress." The ring points to the fidelity that we dream of. Think of the story of Cinderella — the prince is running about the kingdom to find the maiden who owns the glass slipper so he can marry her. Every time I slip my rings on and off, I'm reminded of that. This ring, this symbol of our fidelity, fits me just right. It's a wonder that a small circular piece of jewelry that slides over a finger could hold such a lifetime of promise.

One of our friends, who was part of the young adult

group that used to meet at our home, was out trying on wedding dresses. When she found "the one" she sent me a photo. She was all aglow in the beautiful white gown, and I texted her back. "The way you feel in that dress is the way that God has seen you since the beginning of time."

We maintain that sense of wonder and amazement when we realize how big our God is. You have to sit before something that is greater than yourself and acknowledge your own littleness in order to cultivate this sense of wonder. If you do this enough, even the smallest things, like a butterfly flitting across your yard, will be an occasion of amazement.

How do you maintain that sense of wonder about your husband and your marriage? These questions may help:

- How did you meet?
- What have been moments of grace in your marriage?
- How has God proven his faithfulness to your marriage?
- What lessons have you learned in your marriage, about yourself and together with your husband?

Thanksgiving

"To be a child means to owe one's existence to another, and even in adult life we never

> *quite reach the point where we no longer*
> *have to give thanks for being the person we*
> *are. This means we never quite outgrow*
> *the obligation to give thanks for ourselves*
> *or to continue to ask for our being."*

We must always approach our spouse with a sense of gratitude. The givenness that is included with your identity as spouse is through the relationship with the other. I am spouse because I said yes to him; his reciprocation is what made me wife. This constant state of giving and receiving should be met with thanks.

If we can remain in a state of thanksgiving for our marriage, that gratitude can thwart our complaints, moments of selfishness, and times when we are tempted to cast all blame on the other. You can never outgrow the obligation to say thank you.

We are free and able to receive when we are in a state of gratitude. We look beyond our circumstances and dwell in thanks when we gaze at all that we have been given. So gratitude becomes a foundation for a life of holiness, a life that is not self-centered but one that is other focused, outward focused. Gratitude is necessary for virtue. Likewise, when we turn in, when we practice ingratitude, we become me-focused. We often find ourselves giving into temptation, turning to sin, turning away from God. Ingratitude is the basis for vice. Making thankfulness a way of life is necessary to become child and to become wife.

Mystery

*"Here [in the Church] we discover a new sphere
for the exercise of Christian childlikeness: in the
ecclesial reception of the sacraments authorized
by Christ, in the proclamation of his Word
and in the leadership ordained by Him."*

While the priest is conferred with the power to confect the Eucharist, to forgive sins, to anoint the sick, he only does so by the grace of God. God alone gave us the Eucharist and invites his children to the table. God alone forgives sins and prepares souls for death. Though docile to his will the priest will never grasp the full power of his consent to the Father.

Your life together is a journey toward knowledge of the other, though you'll never reach complete knowledge of him.

Likewise, the consent of the layperson allows something beyond his understanding to become tangible, but not without a childlike reception and belief in the mystery. Certainly, the Eucharist exists without our presence in the pews; but our belief in that which we do not understand allows the Eucharist to be received and, through our consent and holiness, shared with the world. This consent is not one of blind obedience but one of maturity and trust in that which we cannot understand. The lambs follow the shepherd not for lack of knowledge, but for a steady knowledge that he will lead them to the green pastures.

This sense of mystery must be cultivated.

Cultivating mystery in marriage means to realize and find comfort in the fact that you cannot know your spouse totally. Your life together is a journey toward knowledge of the other, though you'll never reach complete knowledge of him.

The sense of mystery also gifts us with a sense of reverence. If you can rest in the mystery of your husband, you can also revere him as someone that is unknown, and yet someone that you cannot wait to continue to know. Dietrich von Hildebrand, a German philosopher, called this reverence an "essential element of every love":

> Reverence for the beloved one is also an essential element of every love. To give attention to the specific meaning and value of his individuality, to display consideration toward him, instead of forcing our wishes on him, is part of reverence. It is from reverence that there flows the willingness of a lover to grant the beloved the spiritual "space" needed to freely express his own individuality. All these elements of every true love flow from reverence. What would a mother's love be without reverence for the growing being, for all the possibilities of value

that yet lie dormant, for the preciousness of the child's soul?

Reverence that maintains space for the other person to be himself allows for the cultivation of mystery. No matter how long you have been married to your husband, he should still surprise you. You should still find yourself exclaiming (hopefully happily), "I never knew that about you!" or "Wow! Just when I thought I knew all there is to know about you, I come to something new!"

You cannot exhaust love. That thought alone is a mystery to be revered!

Take Time as It Comes

> *"The child has time to take time as it comes, one day at a time, calmly, without advance planning or greedy hoarding of time. Time to play, time to sleep."*

It is difficult to run a household with two adults, six children, and a giant dog. There are appointments and play dates, due dates and soccer practices, vet appointments and dinners that must be scheduled. It would be futile to try to achieve any kind of sanity without a schedule, but the times when there is no schedule are cherished and end all too quickly.

Jason and I review the upcoming week every Sunday night. We talk through balancing work and play. Sometimes we even have to schedule "time away." Doing this week to week can become overwhelming and draining. It starts to feel like the schedule that keeps everything afloat is actually selling every moment in advance.

The human heart needs time to recollect, to be without a schedule and without a plan, to simply exist. When we are able to do this as a couple or even as a family, we always walk away feeling loved, feeling free, feeling more like ourselves. I think this is because we are able to give ourselves to the moment without being pulled by the next appointment or task. We are able to be truly present to those around us.

Regardless of what we are doing, I feel most loved when Jason is present with me, and he feels most loved when I am present with him. When we can truly be by one another's side in body and mind and heart, we are able to take each moment as it comes, together. Every second should open itself up into eternity, thereby reminding us that every second is absolutely precious. It cannot be replaced or given back to you.

Our daughter, Abigail, is always concerned with wasting time. It doesn't matter how much time she gets to play or how many warnings she is given that time is ending. Whenever we have to move on to the next thing she always exclaims, "Oh my gosh! We wasted time again!" While it is adorable, there is a sense that her childlikeness is being lost. Children rarely understand the notion of time; it's merely measured by how tired their bodies become.

When we as adults give of ourselves fully to one another or even to a task, at the conclusion there is always a sense of timelessness. There's always the notion of "Where did the time go? It feels like we just started."

Becoming a Childlike Wife

For us to become more and more spouse, we have to give into the childlike traits of embracing wonder, giving thanks, appreciating mystery, and taking time as it comes. In fact, I believe it would strengthen your fidelity and love for your husband to put these traits into practice every single day.

Make time to wonder, to sit in the littleness of your life. What were all the circumstances that led to now? Then, make time to wonder at your marriage. What brought you together? What makes your marriage work? What fills you with joy together?

Never stop saying thank you. Thank God for the morning sun and the darkness of night. Thank him for the air in your lungs and the ground beneath your feet. Do not allow ingratitude to numb you to the graciousness of your very existence! It is good that you exist! Be thankful for that.

Be grateful for your husband and your marriage. Thank him for every moment that he makes you feel special. Thank him for the small things and the giant gestures. Thank him for making you a wife, because while you are not walking toward the marriage altar today, he is still making you a wife as he chooses you again and again today. It's something to be thankful for.

Sit in the mystery of our faith. When you receive the Eucharist, relish in the fullness of that moment and your inability to fully know how great this morsel of bread is that you consume. Remember the moments when your faith was tested and when you returned to the truth. Sit in the unknown moments and allow yourself to feel the weight of that mystery. Do not be afraid. Be content.

Get lost in awe at the sight of your husband's face. He is a mystery that you'll never fully know but that you will never cease to try and know. He desires to be known by you even though you cannot exhaust that knowledge. What a gift to try!

Take time to let time go. Mark off hours or days each month for nothing to be scheduled. Just be, both alone and together with your husband. Be okay with your own existence, with your own being, and it'll make all that planned time even sweeter.

If we dive headlong into becoming more like a child, we will find it easier to be spouse, to be self-gift.

We become wife by continually becoming children.

Acknowledgments

Every single word in this book is the fruit of great love, the love of God, the love of my family, and the love of our dear friends.

Thank you.

To my husband, Jason: What God has placed in my heart you have tended, cared for, and harvested. It's my greatest joy to be loved by you, and you will forever be my favorite.

To my children: Even though this book is about being a wife, within these pages I know that each of you could find guidance for whatever vocation you say yes to. I am so glad that I get to be Gabriel's mom, Jeremiah's mom, Gemma's mom, Abigail's mom, Benedict's mom, and Josephine's mom. Thank you for allowing me to write and for being a constant inspiration to do so. And to Karol Dietrich: We never knew you but I know that your prayers carry us.

To my dad and Melissa: Thank you for your constant love and prayers. Dad, thank you for saying yes to the little baby in that orphanage in the Philippines. You rescued me.

To the best in-laws that anyone could ever pray for, Bruce and Sally: Mom and Dad, thank you from the depths of my heart for all that you have done for us. Thank you for raising such an amazing son, sharing him with me, and providing the constant gift of your parenthood, friendship, prayers, and love.

To Fr. Ivan Olmo, my spiritual father: Thank you for helping me gain the courage to dive into the depths of my heart in order to make it whole.

To my spiritual brother and priest, Fr. Blake Britton: Thank you for the many tears, discussions, prayers, and debates that fostered this book. And for that one time that you let me borrow a book.

To the many friends who have helped shape who I am by always receiving me with love and care, giving me endless wisdom, and encouraging me to reach for the heights. I especially thank members of the School of Humanity, De Fide, the Burrowshire, and the 2022 cohort of the Diocese of Orlando permanent diaconate program.

And to my late mother, Nancy, and stepfather, JB: I miss and love you both so much. You'd be so proud of what the Lord has given me in this world.

When I started to entertain the idea that I would write a book one day, this was the first idea that came to mind after I couldn't find any other books on such a subject! I knew I didn't want to self-publish and didn't think anyone would say yes to a book like this by a writer like me. So I came up with a shorter book proposal with hope that a publisher would say yes to me and not necessarily to the proposal. Perhaps a conversation would begin!

Thank you to Mary Beth Giltner for being that acquisitions editor, for saying yes to me and not to that initial proposal. I'm so thankful that you and OSV gave me the opportunity to write this book.

Thank you to my editor extraordinaire, Rebecca Martin, who worked with me on this project with much patience and incredible care. I have learned so much from you, especially the importance of saving my work in multiple places!

I am forever indebted to the people of the Hildebrand Project, especially Christopher Haley, John Henry Crosby, and Catherine Dugan. You all have no idea how your hospitality toward my mind and soul awakened a part of me that I didn't know existed. Your work has changed the world and has changed me. Thank you.

To Word on Fire Ministries for giving me the space and care to grow in intellect, practice, and written word. To Brandon Vogt, a tremendous friend and a gracious mentor. Thank you for always believing in me.

Thank you to the following friends who contributed to the pages of this book in ways that they likely don't even realize: Fr. Zack Gray, Fr. Harrison Ayre, Sr. Josephine Garrett, Rabbi Mark Gottlieb, Dr. Maria Fedoryka, Dan and Regina Boyd, and to my lovely spiritual daughters. I cannot name you all here but I am so glad I get to be your spiritual mother, friend, and guide.

Thank you to the friends of my soul, whose incredible works helped to mold the words in this book: Cardinal Angelo Scola, Dr. Tracey Rowland, Fr. Paolo Prosperi, Dietrich and Alice von Hildebrand, Adrienne von Speyr, Hans Urs von Balthasar, Pope St. John Paul II, and Pope Benedict XVI.

To God the Father: You've given me much more than I could ever imagine. Grant me the grace to care for it well. May my hunger for you always exceed my reach.

About the Author

Rachel Bulman is an international speaker and author. She has written and hosted a television series for Catholic TV about Eucharistic miracles, and she appears with her family in the show *Meet the Bulmans,* currently airing on the Word on Fire Institute's YouTube channel. Rachel serves on the advisory board of The GIVEN Institute, and in her spare time, she enjoys reading a good book, lifting weights, and perfecting her Old Fashioned cocktail recipe. Rachel has been married for almost fifteen years, and her husband is a permanent deacon and a physician assistant in orthopedics. They have six children, including a set of twins.